C

Memories of an Island Capital
Kingstown, St. Vincent & the Grenadines, W.I.

Cybercom Publishing
Toronto

1

City of Arches
Memories of an Island Capital
Kingstown, St. Vincent & the Grenadines, W.I.

National Library of Canada Cataloguing in Publication Data

Child, Vivian, 1920-
City of arches : memories of an island capital, Kingstown, St. Vincent & the
Grenadines / Vivian Child.

Includes index.

ISBN 0-9731925-5-0

1. Historic buildings--Saint Vincent and the Grenadines--Kingstown. 2. Architecture--Saint
Vincent and the Grenadines--Kingstown. 3. Kingstown (Saint Vincent and the Grenadines)-
-History. I. Title.

F2110.K56C44 2004   972.9844   C2003-906802-1

This edition published by Cybercom Publishing
835 York Mills Rd., # 1135
Toronto, Ontario Canada M3B 1Y2
E-mail: publisher@cybercominc.net

Cover, layout and text design: Tim Harrison
Editor: J. Bentley Harrison
Printed and bound in the United States of America and London, England.

The publisher wishes to express his appreciation to the Vincentian Publishing Company,
Kingstown, St. Vincent & the Grenadines for granting permission to reproduce all or part of
the series of articles on the architecture of Kingstown which were written by Dr. Vivian Child
and originally published in "The Vincentian" Newspaper.

AN INTRODUCTION

Dr. The Honourable Ralph E. Gonsalves
Prime Minister, St. Vincent and the Grenadines.

The heritage, identity and culture of a nation are too often dependent on the collective memories of its citizens, passed down through generations: Memories however are clouded by the passage of time while conflict, human neglect, fire, hurricane, volcanic eruption, earthquake and other catastrophes destroy and erode our monuments, our buildings, our homes and even our people.

We are fortunate to have as one of our National Treasures, a long-time medical practitioner, Dr. Vivian Child. In "City of Arches, Memories of an Island Capital", Dr. Child has frozen time in a series of architectural snapshots. Like a phoenix rising from the ashes, she has created original drawings and paintings of interesting buildings taken of old photographs and from contemporary paintings of buildings as they stand today.

By including historical facts and interesting narrative accounts of Kingstown, the Capital City of the nation of St. Vincent and the Grenadines, "City of Arches", gives us an important historical perspective of the capital, past and present.

I recommend its reading by anyone interested in out multi-island nation. It will captivate our current citizens and residents as well as visitors and tourists who have been here or are planning a visit.

For Vincentians living throughout the world, it will bring back fond memories that might even encourage them to return to their island home.

Dr. Child deserves our appreciation and thanks for preserving this aspect of our history.

It is a significant contribution to the further ennoblement of our Caribbean civilisation and its Vincentian component.

Ralph E. Gonsalves

Dr. The Honourable Ralph E. Gonsalves
Prime Minister,
St. Vincent and the Grenadines.

Come journey with us as we are transported into a charming early 20th century West Indian City. Our tour guide, Dr. Vivian Child, beckons us in her *"City of Arches" Memories of an Island Capital, Kingstown, St. Vincent and the Grenadines, West Indies*, to listen to the walls as we walk through early Kingstown. The arched buildings shading our sidewalks creating a unique tapestry to our urban landscape, the gingerbread houses, the cottages, the beautiful churches, the courthouse, the picturesque roads, even the trees, come alive as families long passed re-emerge from the walls and conduct their day-to-day lives.

Our tour guide is a Vincentian artist, writer, medical doctor and well-known newspaper columnist whose weekly column "Round and About" has been a popular feature for over Twenty years in *The Vincentian*, the national newspaper of St. Vincent and the Grenadines.. In the 1980s, Dr. Child wrote for *The Vincentian* a series of well-researched, illustrative articles on the architectural history of Kingstown. The series was critically acclaimed and stirred up a great deal of interest in architectural preservation. Twenty some years later, Dr. Child has updated and compiled this series in *City of Arches.* as her contribution to preserving the national heritage of St. Vincent and the Grenadines. "The past is history; we cannot change what has been, but we can learn from our successes and our failures. The present is today; by creating a national awareness and sensitivity of our culture and our history, we can preserve our remaining icons of historical significance for the future...Failure to do so will create an unforgivable and irreplaceable loss to future generations," she states.

Today, notwithstanding the present modern architectural evolution in St. Vincent and the Grenadines, the arched buildings still permeate the Kingstown landscape. Several of the buildings that Dr. Child features, though, have been absorbed by modern development. *City of Arches...* gives us a valuable road map, a permanent context, for ensuring that our structures are not arbitrarily destroyed through lack of awareness of their historical value.

Read *City of Arches.* It will at once educate, motivate and entertain you. Most of all, you will be inspired by Dr. Child's unstoppable, pioneering spirit to utilize your own talents to make your best contribution to human civilization.

City of Arches is an invaluable gift to the people of St. Vincent and the Grenadines.

Desiree Richards
Managing Director

Dedicated to
the people of St. Vincent & the Grenadines
with whom I have lived, worked and loved
for over 50 years.

Dr. Vivian Child

Index of Pictures

St. Vincent & the Grenadines
"The Jewels of the Caribbean"

St. Vincent and the Grenadines are located in the West Indies, between the Caribbean Sea and the North Atlantic Ocean, north of Trinidad and Tobago. They are often referred to as "The Jewels of the Caribbean".

The islands were inhabited around 5000 BC by the peace loving Ciboney, then by the Arawaks followed by the war-like Caribs. Throughout time, St. Vincent and the Grenadines has had a colourful and turbulent history.

A Dutch slave ship, wrecked off Bequia in 1675, brought the first Africans, who inter-married to create the Black Caribs, whose descendants live here today. Fought over for nearly a century by the French and British, sovereignty was settled on the British in 1783. Today St. Vincent and the Grenadines is part of the British Commonwealth and an independent democracy.

In Kingstown, the nation's capital, the colonial influence is beautifully captured in its unique architecture, many fine churches, public buildings and interesting homes. The St Vincent Botanic Gardens, founded in 1765, are the oldest in the western hemisphere.
It was here that Captain Bligh, the infamous captain of the Bounty, first brought the breadfruit trees intended to provide food for the slaves.

With the possible exception of Frederickstadt and Charlotte Amalie in the Virgin Islands, the use of arches in the construction of many buildings appears unique to Kingstown, the nation's capital, hence the title: "City of Arches: Memories of an Island Capital, Kingstown, St. Vincent and the Grenadines".

Dr. Vivian Child

During the 1980s, the well known St. Vincent medical doctor, writer and artist, Dr. Vivian Child wrote a popular series of articles for the island's oldest newspaper, The Vincentian. Her intent was to inform her readers about the history and architecture of the more interesting buildings in Kingstown.

She also sketched pictures of the buildings, some as they are today and others from earlier pictures, etchings, drawings and paintings as they were during the late 18th, 19th and 20th centuries. In her articles, she discussed the influence and origin of various architectural designs and where possible, traced the ownership from the time of construction to the 1980s. Her exhaustive research and subsequent writing and illustrations have earned an

Dr. Vivian Child, circa 1950-51

important role in preserving the cultural heritage of the island.

Dr. Child has made her original manuscripts available for publication, working closely with the editors and publisher for accuracy. Because the articles were written in the mid 1980s, they should be read and viewed as a snapshot in time, modified by events, changes and commercial developments during the subsequent 20-25 years.

Sion Lodge 1956

This picture shows the original house as it was until the 1960s when the Anglican Church bought it from the Davis family (whose ownership of a local Kingstown hotel dates back to 1872 or 73). It was converted into a chapel and flats for the clergy and due to a constant battle with termites it was gradually converted from a wood to a concrete building. In this picture, the house was built on a stone foundation and had a shingled roof and a main wooden story with the front door under a decorative gabled veranda. Note the unusual shape of the large sash windows.

The front drive swept around a grassy island with bushes and plants and behind the house is a lofty cabbage palm, which at the time of writing was not easy to see from the road.

While I am unsure of the exact building date, Sion Lodge was originally occupied by Chief Justice Chopping. In 1877, it was purchased by Bequian, John Hercules (founder of Hazells Ltd). He bequeathed it to his son who in turn, left it to his son Percy Hazell, grandfather of Mr. Richard Gunn, a leading member of the merchant community of Kingstown. It was sold to the Davis family in 1940, who subsequently rented it to a religious organization, "Streams of Power".

The Glorious Murray Road, Scenic Route in the City

Early in the 20th century, what is now Murray Road was part of the Frenches Estate. People entering or leaving Kingstown on the southern side had to use the steep Town Hill. Imagine horse-drawn traffic toiling up that road on a rainy day before it was paved!

Large iron gates were closed each night barring entry to the estate at "Frenches Gate" near the present Belingy's store, Frenches Estate was at one time owned by William Smith, grandfather of Mrs. Clara Layne of Laynes Store. He left it to an engineer Clary Smith, who was born in Clare Valley. Smith perished when Chester Cottage, the Estate House was burnt in 1901. A house was rebuilt on the same site, which is on the flat bluff on the side of the present Murray Road adjacent to the present Sally Spring Road. Just below were the Estate works where the University Centre and Craft centre now stand. The Estate works were supplied by waterpower from a branch of the South River, whose water flow in those days was much heavier than today.

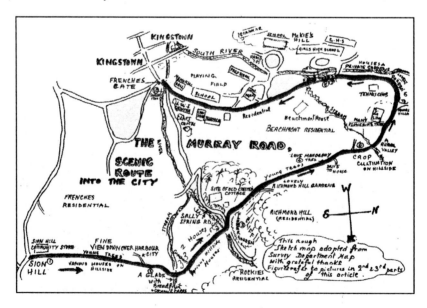

A few years later, the Government bought the entire estate to enlarge the town. Land at Rocky's and Murray Village, which was surveyed by a Mr. Donahue, was sold very reasonably and in some cases actually given to poor people as house spots. Land at Richmond Hill and the area now known as Frenches, below the present Murray Road, was developed as a residential area, where today we see among many shade trees, charming older style houses, mixed with attractive modern ones.

The magnificent Murray Road was created around 1914 and named after Mr. Gideon Murray, a friendly and popular administrator of the island. From the top of Sion Hill it sweeps down along hillsides, gently losing height until it makes a wide hairpin bend by the Tennis Club into town.

Few capital cities can have such an attractive approach as the Murray Hill entrance into Kingstown. On entering Murray Road from the heights of Sion Hill, one is immediately impressed with the panorama of Mount. St. Andrew and the Dragon's teeth mountains, often filtered by filmy clouds. Many do not notice this view, as it quickly gives way to the mass of Richmond Hill with its attractive houses, themselves partially hidden by large trees.

To the left is a fine view of the city and harbour, as the land falls so steeply away that one cannot see the residential area of Frenches just below. The edge of the road has been planted with young plants and trees.

On the right there are well kept houses with nice gardens and retaining walls - contrasted further on with fleeting glimpses of a verdant rustic glade with animals grazing peacefully beneath breadfruit and coconut trees.

The descending road then curves outwards above two "wallhouses" with fine trees, while on the steep upper slopes to the

11

right, we see other houses with pretty gardens built above retaining walls.

The road curves abruptly into the hillside while to the left the shady Sally Spring Road plunges precipitously downward beside a dry wooded gully. Right ahead is a cliff below the heights of Richmond Hill where luxuriant vines fall gracefully over the cliff edge. At its foot is a lovely flower garden created by the Agricultural Department.

Opposite, on the left, is a wide flat bluff with a house built on the site of the old Frenches Estate house, formerly known as "Chester Cottage" and beyond are Kingstown and the harbour.

The road curves around Richmond Hill passing the Croton lined drive that leads up between velvety lawns to Mr. Gonsalves hillside home. Between this lovely house and the road are his immaculate and beautiful "Richmond Hill Gardens".

After passing a beautiful mahogany tree and a wooded uphill driveway, another splendid view of the distant mountains is revealed. It is a surprisingly rural looking hillside planted with crops, and beyond a pleasant house one sees a little grassy valley with a stream and just one cottage. Then on the left is a crowd of trees many of them flowering varieties, including Poinsettias, pink and yellow Cassias, and King of Flowers, each giving a magnificent display in season.

Many of these trees belong to Mr. Silva who left them to shade and decorate his depot of neatly parked cars. This used to be the flower garden of Mr. Fred Hadley's old wooden house now undergoing renovation. Opposite are several attractive homes amidst a mass of Breadfruit and Mango trees where the road to Murray Village leads off uphill to the right.

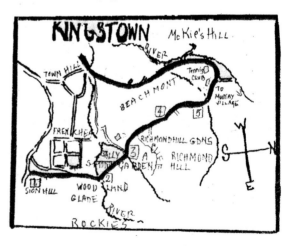

A Gem of a House

Here is an absolute gem of traditional small house architecture. What a joy to see such a charming residence so well maintained! The house is the first to the left on the road that leads steeply up to Rockies from the Murray Road (opposite the Sally Spring Road). The house is romantically situated beside the dramatic cliff that rises from the beautiful garden created by the Forestry

Department. It can easily be seen from the Murray Road with its pale blue walls contrasting with the surrounding large shade trees.

It is not enough however, to admire this side of the house only, because if one climbs the Rockies Road for a few yards the elegant little entrance porch is revealed, set into the angle between two gables. A flight of stone steps decorated with potted plants, leads from the pretty iron work garden gate up to the front door that opens onto the wooden upper story. The miniature gabled roof that shelters the porch is richly decorated with white fretwork that also trims the big gable of the house. The peak of the tiny gable is emphasized with a white ornamental spike. Hanging baskets with beautiful pendulous plants decorate the porch.

13

A rather complex galvanized roof is painted red; the wooden upper story is sky blue with corner trim and window surrounds are of reddish brown. The windows are of a traditional sash windows design and most are flanked in the typical West Indian way by fixed wooden jalousies, painted a deep cream shade.

The house is enhanced by flowering bushes, especially scarlet poinsettias. It is as attractive within as without and has a view of the harbour below.

Mr. Eric Browne, well known as the very helpful boss of P. H. Veira's Lumber Yard, bought the house in 1954. Sometime between 1916 and 1929 it was the property of Frank Marshall who later went to Canada. There have been some alterations in the arrangement of the roof and gables since then and there have been some additions.

The lower part of the house is of stone and has been pleasantly modernised.

Mr. and Mrs. Browne raised their family here, some of whom have emigrated to North America. One of the sons is a member of the St. Vincent Police, a daughter works in the Tourism Department, and another son is a guitarist with the distinctive group known as "Almo".

There are a number of houses of this type scattered about in Kingstown's residential areas. Fortunately some are lovingly kept in beautiful

14

condition, however in some cases they are owned by absentee landlords or by people who find it difficult to pay the high cost of repairs and of paint. Nothing among buildings is sadder than the visible decay of a wooden house formerly bright with paint and lacy white trimmings.

The Murray Road doubles back on itself, around the Kingstown Tennis Club, which moved there in 1955 from a Government owned site in Back Street where the Post Office now stands. Opposite is a pretty little white wooden cottage set amidst breadfruit trees.

Adjoining this house is the golden yellow house of Mr. Lionel Coombs, which is approached by an impressive flight of steps. It was built to Curacao design in the early 1960s and stands amidst colourful gardens on the other side of the little Kingstown South River.

"Beachmont". Built around 1915 by W.H. Beach. 1985.

Continuing on the right are several other attractive homes with private gardens, each approached by its own little bridge over the river, until a public bridge takes the road up McKies Hill.

Beside this bridge, stands a fantastically twisted Eucalyptus tree. Over the bridge is the entrance to the lovely grounds of the Girls High School, with its many flowering trees.

The central house used to be the official residence of the Chief Justice until the mid 1940s, when the school moved from the premises now occupied by the Public Health Department. The old house is built in a style frequently seen in Barbados and superficially resembles Montague House (the Estate House of Grand Sable Estate) behind Georgetown.

Mrs. Moffat was the first Headmistress in this building and occupied the upper part with her retired veteran husband. The school can be easily seen from the Murray Road beyond the fine old trees with their occasional display of yellow blooms, that line each side of the little river until it swerves away behind the grassy "Triangle" in a wooded ravine at the foot of the grounds of the Boys Grammar School.

After passing a small road leading into a residential area there is a walled garden, above which peep brilliant red poinsettias in season, and a white wooden house, called "Shamrock Lodge" built in an unusually steep gabled style by a Mr. O'Donahue. This house used to be the home of Mr. Edwin and Clara Layne and later the home of their son Errol and family.

Beyond this home behind some open land, is the dignified Beachmont House. It is now used for a construction business, but was originally built by William Henry Beach around 1915. Although the style is of an older era, it served as a town residence when he was manager of Mt. Bentinck

Estate. His son became a Surgeon Rear Admiral in the Royal Navy and the house was sold.

After leaving the grassy "Triangle" on the right there is the building of the Ministry of Trade, Industry and Agriculture. This building houses the Forestry Department, the importance of which is becoming ever more evident for the survival of the Nation's agriculture and water supplies.

This Department has also been busy planting ornamental and shade trees of different kinds along the Murray Road. The pictures show the lower part of the road as it looked for many decades up to 1983, when it unfortunately became necessary to cut down the elegant Eucalyptus trees.

These shade trees, an Australian variety, had been planted around 1905 by the Agricultural and Horticultural School which was located on the site of the present Boys Grammar School. It is said that this beautiful tree, with the distinctive pale bark, has an alarming tendency to shed apparently healthy branches at unexpected times! For this reason together with age and its proximity to electric lines the felling was sadly necessary.

Their timber was used to heat the ancient bread oven at Fort Charlotte where prisoners baked bread for the institutions. In a decade or two young trees of different varieties will hopefully have grown up to restore the cool shady appearance of the road.

Although the buildings in the last part of the Murray road are not visually spectacular they are interesting for other reasons. After passing the little road leading towards the Grammar School, on the right a large playing field can be seen behind the Richmond School. In this playing field and the surrounding school buildings, the large Agricultural, Industrial, Craft and Art shows have been held.

Then comes the Memorial Hall built, just after the Second World War as a gift to St. Vincent, by the American firm of "Morningstar" that used to purchase a large proportion of the island's arrowroot starch. Mr. George Muller, their representative, made many visits here and had a great love for St. Vincent and its people. He was probably instrumental in arranging this gift, which has meant so much to the cultural life of the nation. Until recently it was one of the only places for concerts and plays. In 2002 it was beautifully restored.

On the left side of the road, going into town, there are several pleasant homes of gray stone set amidst flower gardens. These were built soon after World War 11. Beyond is a wide pasture, sometimes occupied by sheep, who trim the grass in front of the Technical Centre.

"Save the Children" was opened in 1964 partly as a local day care centre for young children of working mothers, but principally as a school to train Nursery care workers from the different English speaking Caribbean islands. Monica Green was its first director. In 1969 the Canadian branch of the Charity took it over under the name of Canadian "Cansave" and it is now "Vinsave".

The next building is the Extramural Department of the University of the West Indies, referred to as the "University Centre". (A Government cotton ginnery had been built there in the early part of the 20th century, but was destroyed by fire on the same night as the Laynes store fire in 1959.) As the cotton industry declined the ginnery was also used to process copra to make soap and oil. The late Sir Joseph Eustace was its last manager.

The University Centre was built on this site. Some of the ruins can still be seen amidst the landscaping done by Mr. Con de Freitas. There are many beautiful plants one being a Jacaranda tree which displays heavenly blue flowers in season. On an outside wall there is a decorative feature inspired by Vincentian Pre-Colombian petroglyphs (or rock carvings), designed by this writer for a competition and executed by the "Caribee Studios" of Wallilabou, who were famous for their Batik works.

Behind the centre's gardens is a small road, which leads to the Craft Centre, housed in aged estate or ginnery buildings. Behind the Craft Centre is a neat modern building where the Agro Lab used to produce edible delicacies from local produce.

We then come to an enormous spreading Saman tree beside a stream lined with pretty riverside plants. Enjoy the sight of it while you may; I am concerned for its future.

After leaving this tree and another side road we reach "Trenches Gate", the location of the heavy iron gates that closed off Frenches Estate every sunset before construction of the Murray Road.

Kingstown Waterfront

This part of the Kingstown waterfront is as it was in the 1950s and well before the Harbour Reclamation in the late 1960s. At the time of the photo all the buildings were plastered and washed in various pale colours. The long building on the extreme right belonged to Casson and was occupied by Coreas. It was white and the practical window hoods were painted bright blue. The arched arcade below

extended around the corner into Egmont Street.

The next building was occupied at that time by the firm of Hilary Da Silva & Son. Later, prior to being completely destroyed by fire in 1983, it was occupied by Edwin Layne and Sons as a hardware store. The next building, also destroyed in the same fire, was occupied by Coreas and later as a wholesale outlet by Low Budget Supermarket. The second last building also belonged to Coreas and the building on the extreme left, is now Sprott Bros., "Home Works".

The upstairs windows have subsequently been altered and the plaster has been removed to reveal the attractive brickwork beneath. The bricks, seen in so many of our old buildings, are said to have been brought mainly as ballast in the hold of the ships that came over to pick up the island's sugar exports.

The beach, with small boys playing in the waves, adjoins Bay St., where you can see boats and gasoline drums. This was also before the Harbour Reclamation Scheme.

An attentive observer will notice in this street scene, that the individual buildings while all slightly different, blend together in harmony, and they all conform to the distinctive Vincentian styles.

Two Famous Hotels

This is a view of two well-known buildings as they remain to this day. On the left is the Blue Caribbean Building, which was constructed sometime between 1919 and 1928. It was for some years the "Pelican Hotel" owned by Herbert Davis (father of Mrs. E. Crosier), who had operated his hotel in the house that is now the Public Works building in Back St., and later on the site of the present Caribbean Banking Corporation.

A one-story building had earlier occupied this site which then belonged to Mr. Porter, owner of a great deal of town property, plus twenty four estates including Orange Hill, during the early twentieth century.

In the 1940s Mr. Claude Layne purchased the Hotel and completely reconstructed the entire building, using the traditional Kingstown style architecture to make a solid stone and concrete structure. In 1949 it was reopened as the "Blue Caribbean Hotel". His wife Ossie was the manager.

In 1976, after Mr. Layne's death, the retirement of his wife and the emigration to Australia and Canada of his children, the building was turned into offices and shops for rent. The arched arcade of the ground floor, which had been enclosed as a sitting out place for guests, was opened to the public as a pedestrian thoroughfare. It has been painted a bright blue, which does much to liven up the scene. The next time you pass by, notice the curved hoods over the dignified Georgian type sash windows.

To the right was the "Heron Hotel". The upper story was constructed mainly of wood with a projecting wooden balcony and was painted a pretty shade of pink. Alongside the building flows the little South River below the little bridge, which can be seen in the photo. For 2-3 decades the hotel which adopted the name "Southbridge", was run by the three Grant sisters.

The charming building which dates from the last half of the nineteenth century resembled the old West Indian style seen in other islands. In 1905, it was bought by Mr. Walter Barnard of St. Lucia, who also acquired Orange Hill Estate from Mr. Porter. It had been completely devastated by the 1902 Souffriere eruption. Barnard is said to have bought it for sentimental reasons to please his wife Ida, who had been raised there.

Mr. Barnard used the building as a town house at a time when horse transport made travelling a slow business in St. Vincent. He died in England in the 1919 World Influenza Pandemic.

The building was rented out as a hotel until The Barnard Family took it back and renamed it the "Heron Hotel".

Although much renovated, it still retained all the charm of an old style West Indian town house with the balcony and its cool interior courtyard full of exotic greenery, until it fell victim to termites and was demolished in 2002.

Visitors Enjoy the cool Vincie style arcades

There will scarcely be a visitor who does not at sometime during his or her stay, stroll along Bay Street on its cobbled pavement, protected from the sun and rain by this typical arcade which houses some very interesting shops.

In the foreground is part of the long arched arcade of the Blue Caribbean building. We then come to the well-known department store of Edwin D. Layne and Sons. The arches on this building were replaced by pillars some years ago following a disastrous fire.

The next three buildings also have lovely arches. Moving along, we come to the charming "Cobblestone Inn" reconstructed by Robin Hazell, A few years ago the plaster was stripped from these three buildings to reveal the old pinkish brown brickwork beneath.

Beyond these three was another arched building, which was destroyed by fire in the 1940s and replaced by a "modern" building supported by pillars. It is rented by the Trinidadian jewellery and furniture store Y. De Lima at the time of writing.

You will notice some new arches in the modern buildings on the opposite side of the street on the Reclamation site. In the English and French speaking Caribbean no other town boasts these long arched arcades except Frederickstadt and Charlotte Amalie in the Virgin Islands, where the arches are differently styled and the arcades are narrower.

There are several other arcades in Kingstown. On a Saturday morning all are thronged with Vincentians constantly stopping and chatting with their friends and acquaintances.

Branching off is a short but attractive street

This picture shows Egmont St. a few years ago. It is of special interest as it shows the first self-service grocery store in St. Vincent, (the forerunner of the supermarkets). The "KWIK SHOP" as it was called, was started by United Traders Ltd. (It subsequently changed hands and became part of Corea's Trading). It was housed in the attractive location depicted here, and remains essentially unchanged.

The illustration shows the view through the arches of Trotman's lovely building, which has since been stripped of its plaster and whitewash to reveal its mellow brick construction.

Beside the "KWIK SHOP" you can see a dull shed-like building that has now been replaced with a handsome structure with a gallery.

In the distance there is a glimpse of the Thomas' building, at that time rented by U.T.L. (Coreas) with its long arched arcade; all sadly destroyed by fire in later years.

This picture is from a period before the Harbour reclamation so that the sea can be seen nearby. The reclaimed land was soon covered with fine buildings.

Egmont St 1955

Charming Old Egmont Street

This sketch shows a part of Egmont St. looking inland. The elegant arched arcade in the foreground is a building belonging to Trotman's Electronics Ltd. Mr. Trotman purchased it from the Sprott family, who had owned it for many years together with adjoining buildings. Its age is not known, but it is thought to have been built by Mr. James Elliot Sprott. It is probably over one hundred years old.

Mr. Sprott died relatively young after being nominated as a member of the then Legislative Council. He owned and edited the newspaper The "Rambler", which was noted for interesting comments and informative stories. The "Rambler" was later replaced by his newspaper, "The Sentry."

The building was rented out to various businesses, including the Grenadian firm of T. R. Evans which ran a dry goods store on the ground floor under the management of Mr. Cox. Mrs. Rampersaud occupied part of the ground floor site with a beautiful jewellery shop. Another part of the ground floor was rented by the first of the offshore banks to be set up in St. Vincent.

During the late 1960s Mr. Trotman purchased the property, renovated the building and removed the plaster from the facade to reveal an attractive, pinkish brown brickwork.

Opposite, was a long old building with a wooden upper story painted a gleaming white. It was owned by Mrs. Nanton, and had shops below and many smart boutiques above. It has since been replaced.

In the distance, Singers Building can be seen. It replaced a building that was very similar to the Nanton building, with a similar wooden upper story which continued up to the corner of Back St. It belonged to Mr. Lisle Gill, who demolished it replacing it with a more modern structure.

Gone With The Flames

This used to be my favourite Kingstown building. It was sadly destroyed by fire in1981. The fire was thought to have started in a small upstairs restaurant. It stood on the busy corner of Bay St. and Egmont St. opposite what was once J. H. Hazell's large store (Groceries Supermarket, etc.), rented by Y De Lima since 1974.

The sketch shows only the Egmont St. side. This is adjacent to the long main Bay St. frontage that faced the sea. It had seven hooded sash windows upstairs and five wide, oval arches below that formed part of the long arcade that still continues its cool and shady way as far as the Central Police Station. I especially loved this corner because of the view through multiple arches, beyond which the deep blue sea with ships could be seen.

Although the building was just as depicted right up to the time of the fire, the environs were different before the Harbour Reclamation work of 1971 filled in the nearby sea. Some people tell me that there were only three arches on this side but a study of fragmentary old photos suggests to me that there were four narrow arches and three windows above.

An earlier fire practically destroyed the entire building back in 1925 when Mr. George Corea lived above and conducted a business below. Afterwards he rebuilt or renovated it, retaining or copying the style of the former building with its arched arcade and sash windows. It was undoubtedly he who completely changed the roof from four steeply pitched gables facing the sea, to a style more often seen at present. These pitched gables can be seen in the background of an old photograph of the waterfront taken in 1905. His son, Frederick Augustus Casson, (he changed the family name) continued Corea's business there. He owned a number of estates including Peter's Hope, Mt. Wynne and Arnos Vale where he later made his home in the big house on the hill overlooking the cane fields, later a racetrack and now the Airport.

Some years after his death during the 1950s and 1960s his entire family gradually emigrated to different countries. The widow of one of them donated a large amount of her inheritance to the Government of St. Vincent, at the time of Independence, in order to benefit the new Nation. Her funds helped to build Marian House in the year 2000.

The business was transferred to a large Barbadian firm, Goddards, said to have been founded a generation ago by an enterprising member of a poor Barbadian "Redleg" family. They leased the building from the Casson family and continued to run it as a flourishing grocery business with many important business activities and agencies upstairs.

In 1978, Goddards relinquished their lease and continued the business under the name of Corea's Trading Co. in different premises. Geddes Grand bought the far end of the Bay St. frontage and Mr. Vincent Thomas bought the part of the building shown in the sketch. A wholesale grocery business was run there until the 1981 fire. In the picture you may notice the elderly woman wearing the typical old-fashioned costume that could still be seen before the 1980s.

Another Fire in the City

The tragic fire that occurred early in July 1989 destroyed valuable documents and passports etc. at the Police Immigration Department as well as three lawyer's offices, the premises and merchandise of two popular business enterprises, as well as one of the most charming, harmonious and typical groups of arcaded town buildings in the whole of Kingstown.

The fire consumed half of the block between the Police Headquarters and Egmont St. The other half had been burnt down in 1983, and up to now, only Geddes Grant's new building has risen loftily from the ruins.

The above sketch is taken from a photograph I took way back in the 1950s long before the harbour reclamation scheme of the late 1960s. I feel no apology is needed for reminding readers again of how the block used to look; even then I had to lament the loss of Corea's premises, burnt flat in 1983. Located on the right of this picture, it is a large whitewashed brick structure with seven Georgian style sash windows shaded by bright royal blue hoods upstairs facing the sea. The graceful arcade of rather flattened arches continues around the corner along one side of Egmont St.

You will notice the sea lapping on a gray sand beach with piles of wood and other debris that floated right up to Bay Street.

Next to Corea's is another elegant building also occupied by Corea's & Co. and also burnt in that 1983 fire. This has been replaced by Geddes Grant Ltd.'s modern building, which has fortunately continued the tradition of an arched arcade, though the arches are wider and of thinner construction.

Next comes the premises of Hilary Da Silva & Son, which was later occupied by Edwin Layne and Sons Hardware and suffered greatly in that same awful fire. It is currently under reconstruction. (Although I have depicted all the shuttered upstairs windows in the block as open for the sake of appearance, they were actually nearly always closed because behind them were the stockrooms, sometimes filled by use of a ladder entering the longer window openings and sometimes by hauling up the goods through a trapdoor in the floor from the arched gallery below).

The adjacent building was also occupied by Corea & Co. Later it became the Low Budget Supermarket during which time the large glassless upstairs shuttered windows were replaced by lacy decorated concrete blocks. Later this building housed the Key Foods Store until the recent fire. This building had the roundest arches. Although all the buildings harmonised well, there were slight differences between them.

Then came a building with an unusually shaped roof, although older pictures show this type of roof to have been quite prevalent along Bay Street at the turn of the last century. This attractive structure became the site of the excellent "Homeworks", opened by the Sprott Bros. in 1977. It was full of all the useful and decorative items anyone might want in their home as well as clothes, toys and garden tools and ornaments. The owners had given the

28

place a face-lift and had stripped off all the plaster coating to reveal the old brickwork beneath, This building, together with the adjacent "Key Food" building, were completely destroyed in the fire of July '89, as was the Police Immigration Department with the Police Commissioner's Office above on the other side. The latter is not shown in this sketch.

The city of Kingstown is changing constantly and there are many exciting improvements occurring especially on the Reclamation site. I hope that this block of buildings along Bay St. will be rebuilt in a style similar to unique Kingstown style similar to what it was before. No other town in this part of the world has architecture quite like it, although in St. Croix and St. Thomas there are streets made beautiful and distinctive by arched arcades, which differ slightly from ours.

This architecture should be jealously guarded and appreciated. Even if local inhabitants and merchants may not always appreciate their worth at first, they are definitely an asset from a tourist perspective and would eventually become a source of pride to our citizens and increased revenues to the owners.

One can only hope that planners and architects will respect local style and make sensitive reconstruction designs, perhaps improved by inner walkways and court yards that will help to make Kingstown one of the most charming and individual cities of the Eastern Caribbean.

This picture is a photocopy of an old photograph lent to me, courtesy of Miss Ruby Nanton. I have highlighted the image in a few places.

I expect that everyone who has been to St. Vincent can recognize the locality, although it is now vastly changed. The photograph was taken around 1905. At that time, as can be seen, there were fine trees along Bay Street beside the beach on which were drawn up numerous boats. It will be remembered that in those days many people from the leeward side of the island, as well as people coming from the Grenadines travelled by boat to Kingstown.

I am told that the trees were Jumbie trees. They were felled in the 1930s on the advice of the Health Inspector who seems to have imbued a whole generation with a mistrust of trees near habitations, not so much for reasons of safety in bad weather, but for "Health" reasons!

Alas, they were not replanted, so that Kingstown has somewhat of a dry hot appearance compared to some other tropical towns. In a parallel case all the trees along the beach in front of Port Elizabeth in Bequia were felled in the late 1950s and it was some years after the Police and Government were exposed to the full heat of the afternoon sun, that new trees were planted. They have now grown up to give a beautiful appearance and much needed cooling shade to Port Elizabeth.

In Kingstown we have had the Reclamation Scheme since the mid sixties, which will hopefully be developed in a suitably decorative and useful way to enhance, as well as to enlarge, our capital city.

It is interesting to look at the buildings in this old picture. Where the immigration office now stands there is a grim looking gate and wall. Then comes a small one-story building with donkeys outside, which is now part of Sprott Bros. It has had an upper story added and the old iron pillars have been replaced with bricks.

The next building is also occupied by Sprott Bros. Ltd. The roof is much the same shape as it was, but interestingly enough, the roofs of all the other buildings in the block have been changed to a completely different shape.

One can only wonder why that should be. In the distance can be seen the arcaded building that was burnt down recently at the corner of Egmont Street.

Beyond that building is the old Hazells building, before it was burnt down back in the 1940s. It was replaced by a new building, handsome in its way, but of an alien style considered "modern" at the time. This building is, at the time of writing occupied by Y De Lima & Co.

The Former Police Jetty with Rescue boats

This picture is a combination of two old photographs kindly sent to me by the High Commissioner for the Eastern Caribbean States. Probably they date from around 1910. In the foreground is a very neat, wide jetty of wooden boards, complete with old fashioned streetlights.

An important feature is the two small boats that hang in slings out over the water from davits, in the little boathouses on each side of the jetty. Until the end of the 1960s the beach ran all along one side of Bay Street, until it was changed by the Harbour Reclamation Scheme.

Much earlier there was a proper Leeward Highway. Even up to the 1940s, people travelled from the Leeward side of the island in small boats, some of which you can see pulled up on the beach. Sometimes overloaded boats would capsize in rough seas when they rounded Old Woman's Point on their way into Kingstown Harbour. A watch was kept at Fort Charlotte and a cannon would be fired

31

when a boat overturned. This was the signal for the Harbour Police to quickly launch these small boats from under their boathouses and go to the rescue of the people in the unfortunate craft.

At some time the jetty was replaced by a concrete one of much narrower dimensions and a building was constructed beside it in which the police used to practice band music until the middle of 1985. The building is now in disrepair and the jetty is surrounded by the Reclamation site.

The impressive Police Central Headquarters, believed to have been built in the 1890's, remains the same except for slight differences in roofing material and in the present colour of the wooden fixed window jalousies and the red colour of the elegant tower. There have also been some additions at each end.

The building is of neatly cut stone with corner quoins and window surrounds of golden coloured brick. All the windows have fixed jalousies. These windows were painted darkly (green probably) at the time of the pictures. The downstairs windows have elegant arched tops. All the windows are surmounted by alternate groups of red and golden brick. Just under the roof there is an attractive course of bricks sticking out in a saw tooth effect. All these little details are well worth noticing and also the pretty lacey metal ventilators above each upstairs window. Most of these details are too small to show in this drawing.

On the left you can see the bridge, now rebuilt in a more elegant fashion, through Market Square over a drain. I do not know what the building above it was. In the far distance can be seen the arched gates to the Courthouse yard.

Notice the tree on the beach and the many trees behind. Then you can see the De Passos building (later occupied by Bata's Shoeshop). On the hill behind the Central Police Headquarters there is a house, formerly the strategically placed official residence of the Chief of Police, but now occupied by the Ministry of Health. Another tree can be seen by the beach on the right. All the trees along the beach were cut down in the 1930s.

Vanished buildings and trees

I must thank Claudius Thomas, High Commissioner for Eastern Caribbean States in London for sending me the interesting photograph of the market square.

This sketch, which depicts the waterfront of the market square, is from an old postcard lent to me by Miss Ruby Nanton. She thinks it dates from about 1910. It wasn't until the 1960s that this part of the sea was filled in to create the Reclamation land.

Drawn up on the beach are numerous fishing boats with sails from Bequia, and many canoes and rowing boats from the Leeward coasts. On the left is the fish market building in much the same place as it is at present. Then comes the long building occupied for many years by P. H. Veira and rebuilt by that firm a few years ago, in a different and taller style. At the time of the picture, this building belonged to the Joseph family.

The next building is recalled with much affection by those persons familiar with it. It was the Kingstown Board Building and was much admired. It was constructed of red brick, trimmed with white corner quoins and window surrounds. The Town Board offices with their arched push out windows were upstairs, approached by an outside flight of steps opposite the P. H. Veria building. Sadly, this charming edifice was demolished in the early 1950s to make room for a huge Arcon roofed, gray market building.

Next you see a part of a pretty arched building, with sash windows above. I have not been able to determine what the primary use of this building was, however the large building to the right, with its pleasing proportions and elegant doors was part of the market where fish was sold, although some say that it stabled the horses that drew the Town Board garbage carts. Notice the shade trees on the beach and behind the buildings.

A Complete Change in Appearance of the Market Square

Here are two sketches adapted from photos taken looking west from the de Passos part of Jax's Enterprises around 1900 and 1985 respectively. Few readers will recognize that these two sketches are both of the same place. The only constant feature is the wide, deep concrete drain that runs under a flat bridge that carried Middle Street water through the middle of Market Square.

As can clearly be seen in the 1900 sketch, the market used to be conducted under two long shelters of curved black galvanised roofing and some trees. The shelter on the right was later filled in with a row of little shops. It was burnt down in the 1970s and replaced with a more attractive building to house the shops. In this 1985 sketch you cannot see the shelter, because it is hidden by the large electrical transformer, which will soon undergo a beautifying face-lift.

In the 1985 sketch on the extreme left can be seen part of the Ice House, originally built by the Government, sometime in the 1920s. For many years it has been owned by the De Nobriga family but it too disappeared during recent renovations.

In the 1950s the Government built the immense functional gray, "Arcon" roofed market building which replaced the other shelter, trees and some other smaller buildings (not shown). It was demolished in the 1990s and has been replaced with a large modern building.

In the other sketch of 1900 or thereabouts, a long building of dressed stone with many sash windows can be seen on the left at the back. It extended all the way from Bay Street to Lower Middle Street. This used to belong to the Joseph family and later to P. H. Veira and it housed grocery and other businesses. In the late 1970s it was rebuilt in a simple style with an extra story. The bulk of the market shed hides this new building in the small sketch.

A pretty little tower with a pointed roof, similar to the tower that graces the Police Headquarters, can be seen in what used to be the Williams building in Lower Middle Street.

It was replaced by Bonadie, who acquired the building for his supermarket, rebuilding in 1978 on that site and the adjoining site at the corner of Lower Middle Street and Market Square.

This new building has an extra story and its proportions match those of the nearby Veira building. In the 1900 picture, the older building stands in its place. Built in the traditional Kingstown style, it has a graceful and practical arched arcade supporting a brick upper story and it was occupied by the merchant Thomas Lawer.

This building burnt down and was replaced by a similar whitewashed building, but the arches disappeared and a little roof was built out over the pavement supported by flimsy pillars. It was the business premises of the Richards Bros. who lived at "Sunningdale" on Kingstown Park. Later it became the property of Hadley Bros., who demolished the roof and pillars and in the 1970s sold it to Vivian Bonadie.

In the large old sketch it is worth noticing the neat cobblestone of the bridge and the dark jackets, so unsuitable to our climate, worn by the men lounging there. The voluminous dresses of the women are interesting; some of them clearly showing the bunching up of the belt or girdle, a typical feature of traditional West Indian female attire. This feature was still to be seen sometimes as late as the 1950s, even though skirts had become shortened following the 1914-1918 War.

The de Passos House

This very fine house at Lot 109 on the Market Square was purchased by Mr. Antonio de Passos in 1887 and has remained in the possession of the de Passos family ever since. Its present owner, Harris de Passos of New Jersey estimates the house to be over 100 years old. During the early part of the 20th Century, a firm called Thomas Lawer & Co. occupied the ground floor.

The house has the widest arched arcade in Kingstown, providing a very generous shelter for many small traders to display their wares. It is built in the traditional style of dressed stone with brick corner quoins and surrounds, to windows and arches.

Very attractive dormer windows can be seen in the roof. Look closely at their design and decoration, which is unfortunately a bit difficult to make out now that the glass has been painted white. The building was occupied by the famous international shoe selling and manufacturing firm of "Bata". A few years later it became the property of Jax's Enterprises. While preserving the ground and first floors, he made the building into a tall department store. Thus the pretty little dormer windows vanished. The first escalator in St Vincent was installed in Jax's new store.

An Elegant Balcony

This picture shows a charming little building adorned with a balcony with wrought iron railings of unusual and graceful design. This structure was in the courtyard behind the de Passos building in Market Square, when it was occupied by Bata Shoes.

I. Child.   HOUSE IN COURTYARD

Residence of Mr. Jonathon Knight

This house built in the classic Kingstown style on Bay Street is now a business place facing the Harbour Reclamation area. It was built in the 1940s as a residence by Mr. Jonathon Clarke son of the owner of Liberty Lodge Estate (which was subdivided and sold a number of years ago). At that time the beach extended right up to the edge of Bay Street. Mr. Leon Clarke remembers to this day transporting the stone for this house from the quarry in his truck, the "Susanna". The random bare stone masonry of the upper story is different from the neatly dressed stone work seen in earlier homes. There are three traditional dignified sash windows in the hoods. The three beautifully proportioned arches below, supporting the upstairs stone gallery, are smoothly plastered and painted in a rich shade of pink. There are several houses of almost identical stone design scattered about in different streets of Kingstown.

After Jonathan Clarke's death his family continued to reside in the house until emigrating to England when the house was rented out to tenants, one of whom was a Mr. Cardan Knights, who is related to the Clarke family. He used it as a business premise until he purchased it in 1985.

The house partly seen in the sketch to the left, belongs to Mr. Dennis Frank. It is a combined business, warehouse and residential property.

Mr. Frank owned it for about thirty years, purchasing it as an old house with a decaying upper wooden story. Twenty or more years ago he completely renovated it, replacing the gallery with a concrete structure with a more modern type of window. Earlier in the twentieth century, this house, which extends back a long way, was a Town yard, with its many rooms (about twenty) was occupied by different families, each with eight or more children! (This was in an era when Family Planning was unheard of). The present renovated structure is painted in a cheerful shade of golden yellow.

A King Lived Here

This sketch shows some attractive old houses built in the nineteenth century on Melville St. On the left are the two houses that comprised the Gonsalves Liquor Store in the 1980s. They are two fine examples of a characteristic and special style of traditional Kingstown architecture. The first one is of dressed stone construction with "ballast" brick quoins at the corners and brick around the windows and arches. These buildings have had extra stories added to the original structure.

The second house is smaller and is neatly plastered and painted. Both houses belonged to Mr. Joseph the father of the late Miss Ruby Joseph.

The exact year in which these houses were built is hard to determine. Houses of that type appear to have been built during most of the nineteenth century. The first house holds special interest because at one time King Jaja (ex-King of Opobo) lodged there. He had been exiled to St. Vincent from Africa, arriving on the HMS Icarus in 1888. Whilst in St. Vincent he occupied various residences starting with the Fort cottage, which he found too cold.

Many readers will already know about this remarkable man from reading E. J. Alagoa's book, "Jaja of Opobo" (published by Longmans or from Kirwin Morris' article, "King Jaja's exile to St Vincent Flambeau".)

King Jaja was born in 1821 and when a child, became a slave (through kidnapping) to other Africans in Bonny, at a river mouth on the coast of Nigeria. As a young man he distinguished himself sufficiently in the commercial undertakings of the mercantile family to whom he now belonged, that he was made chief of a powerful trading company, Anna Pepple House 1863. In 1870, for various reasons he moved his establishment from Bonny to nearby Andoni at the mouth of the River Imo and founded the state of Opobo, where trade flourished under his leadership.

He controlled extensive trading up the river, but forbade foreigners to engage in any trading, other than with him. He was a good friend to the British Queen Victoria, who recognised him as King of Opobo. His great success and trading enterprise caused his undoing.

In the "Scramble for Africa", that occurred in the nineteenth century among the European powers, the British themselves wanted to trade on the river. This disagreement along with others with King Jaja caused trouble.

King Jaja was tricked against his better judgment to go on a British ship for "trial" in Accra (Gold Coast), where he was found guilty of failing to cooperate in various technical ways with the British attempt to set up a "Protectorate", and with their inland trading plans. He was sentenced to be exiled for at least five years and was given the choice of several different exile locations. He chose St. Vincent.

He was transported to St. Vincent as a political prisoner and allowed a pension of Ł800 annually, which was worth considerably more then than now. His son and one attendant accompanied him.

He appealed his conviction to Queen Victoria, but the appeal was rejected. When his health failed in 1891, he was allowed to return home, but unfortunately died on his way to Tenerife. King Jaja's body was taken back to Opobo, and after a royal funeral lasting thirty days he was buried in his Palace. Later even European traders joined with local people to build a monument to his memory.

Middle Street divided this house from the long attractive old house belonging to Mrs. Da Silva, formerly a dwelling house, that is now a business place. It is an example of an old house with a decorated wooden open balcony, as seen in towns throughout the English speaking West Indies. While similar houses date from about 1820, the exact date of the building of this house is unknown. It was replaced by a modern building around the turn of the century.

There are also some interesting looking new buildings under construction in the nearby section of Middle St. that are worth seeing.

The Salvation Army Blends Past and Present

THE SALVATION ARMY   V.H.Gild

The left side of this well known building in Melville St. has been occupied by the Salvation Army for at least ninety years. The windows have been changed to glass louvres. In 1975 a new wing was added. It was partly funded by "Oxfam" to house the School Feeding Programme, a project dear to the heart of that great lady,

Brigadier Clementina Leopold, who for many years worked for the Salvation Army.

It is pleasing to see how this new wing harmonises with the older building. Its arcade has been enlarged with arches of the same size as the three already under the old building. Upstairs an open area with a balustrade of decorative cona blocks connects the two buildings. The new building has a facing of neatly cut stone. In this building more than two hundred needy children are fed daily in the face of ongoing costs which are constantly rising.

Some Dignified Houses in Higginson Street

Higginson Street is a quiet and dignified residential street, running from Back Street past the end of the Methodist Church towards the reclamation site and down to the sea. Here were two charming houses worth noticing.

The nearer house is thought to have been built some time before 1935, by a Mr. Clarke. It had a white painted wooden upstairs gallery trimmed with dark red paint around the windows and at the corners. As is usual in old houses in Kingstown, a wooden upstairs gallery was supported by plain pillars. The characteristic arches of Kingstown are usually only seen where the upstairs gallery is of heavier material such as stone or brick so that they definitely served a practical purpose.

In the right of this sketch you can see part of the adjacent building, which has recently been rebuilt by the present owner Mr. Moses. It is a good example of the typical contemporary Vincentian style of randomly placed stone masonry, which has been used to good effect. At one time, a lady known as Mother Frances lived there. Succeeding owners included a Mr. Bonadie and Mr. Ford of the Cooperative bank.

The next house, with its traditional arched arcade, belonged to the father of Mr. Ira Young who spent his school days there, and in 1951 founded "Valu-electrical Service", which is indeed a valuable asset to the island. The building was sold to Mrs. Llewellyn.

Moving along, we come to a particularly handsome building, which is unfortunately in very poor condition. It was owned by now deceased Mr. Anderson, who was the author of the much sought after, but out of print "St. Vincent Handbook", which was published before the first World War.

His grandson, the well-known musician, writer and civil servant Kirwin Morris is the present absentee owner. The building

44

was constructed sometime in the early nineteen hundreds in the traditional Kingstown style. It had an arched arcade below, supporting a stone upstairs gallery with three elegant sash windows. This house is unusual in the way the stone has been faced with very neat deep grooves creating an attractive effect resembling that seen at the old Library. The arcade hides an adjacent small house, which stands on the corner of Middle Street.

Beyond Middle Street the Kingstown Anglican School can be seen. It has a decoration edging its large gable. Beyond the school is the wide Reclamation Site between the town and the sea.

Home of Bertram Richards on North River Road

This sketch shows the charming home of Mr. Bertram Richards in North River Road, which runs inland from the Grenville Street end of Back Street between the Roman Catholic Co-Cathedral of the Assumption and the large church yard of the Anglican St. George's

Cathedral, continuing over the crossroad with a bridge to the left (North). The house is painted gleaming white and has a wooden upper story above a masonry lower part. The three upstairs sash windows are protected from the weather by attractive dark green hoods with scalloped edges.

The gable is decorated with pretty white fretwork or what the Americans call "Ginger Bread". There is a small projecting gallery downstairs, protected by breeze-blocks, which harmonise well with the fretwork above. Below the blocks is a wait of random stonework The whole building is slightly narrower than it appears in the drawing.

The house is believed to be about 90 years old and was probably built by Mr. Randolph Richards, who had been an altar boy at the Anglican Cathedral to which he devoted his entire life, serving as verger and performing numerous other essential services.

His son Mr. Bertram Richards was the Principal of the Intermediate High School, which he took over from the Eustace Brothers and continues to run as a successful institution at the other end of the city.

Gaily Painted Old Houses

Rose Place is a wide side street leading from the Hospital end of Greenville Street (Back Street) directly down to the sea. A number of fishing boats, painted in bright colours, are drawn up on the beach where fishermen gather to mend nets and socialise under the grateful shade of recently planted trees.

There are at least three brightly painted houses in this short wide street, which are well seen when leaving the sea and facing inland towards the green mountains. The two houses depicted here are neatly painted. The wooden upper story and veranda of the house on the left were painted in a rich shade of blue, whilst the plastered masonry of the ground floor is painted in a bright golden yellow, with blue-gray wooden doors framed in the dark red of the 1980s.

The building was originally constructed for Thomas Palmer, a Scottish tailor, who came to St. Vincent sometime in the nineteenth century. He is the author of a book, available in the Public Library that describes his adventures at sea when adrift in a small ship, where he had to drink the blood of two turtle doves to keep himself alive! This man brought over a European Almond tree which flourished in his back yard and was decorated every Christmas until it died recently of old age and had to be felled. This sort of Almond tree has nuts, that after shelling taste and look similar to those of the West Indian Almond tree, but there the resemblance ends, as the tree differs in shape and foliage and is distinguished by a cloud of beautiful pink blossoms. Unlike the West Indian Almond tree it is seldom found alongside beaches.

The son of Thomas Palmer, who was also named Thomas, became a shipbuilder as did his son, Hamilton who lived from 1914 to 1983. Ships are still built from time to time on the nearby beach. The house has a wide upstairs veranda, which was added later. The balustrade used to be of delicate lathe turned banisters, but these have been replaced with a much simpler balustrade of crossed pieces of wood.

The next house, of similar shape and size but with a gabled red roof, was also built by a Scottish tailor named Wilson. Like its neighbour, it acquired its balcony at a later date. In the late 1940s Mr. Fred John, an ex-Sergeant Major in the St. Vincent Police, who later became St. Vincent's first Public Assistance Officer, bought the house from Mr. Newsom Duncan, a business man. Fred John was the father of the lawyer Dr. Kenneth John, famous for his regular articles in the "Vincentian" newspaper and also for an earlier popular radio programme, "Searchlight".

The upper story has been painted an attractive aqua colour, and has a white balcony balustrade of a more complicated ends cross design. The lower story of masonry is painted a pale cream trimmed with reddish brown. The house has since been sold and is now rented to people who run a bar on the ground floor.

Opposite these houses is a one of a different but still traditional design, newly painted in a most pleasing shade of rose pink. It is a pity that paint is so expensive in this house-proud nation, otherwise we might see many more cheerful colours among its wooden homes.

Beginning of the Leeward Highway 1980
Houses old and not so old near the Hospital

When proceeding up the Leeward Highway most of us are in too much of a hurry to notice these houses, two of which still existed until just a few years ago.

The one on the right stood on the corner where the road from Victoria Park joins the Leeward Highway. It was there until 1980 when its aging deterioration necessitated its replacement by a pleasant modern concrete cottage of similar size. The owner is Mrs. Lucille Bibby, a fine elderly woman, whose mother built the original house depicted in this sketch over one hundred years ago. It was a most attractive example of a typical Vincentian cottage or superior chattel house of wood on stone foundations. It had the characteristic feature of a dignified sash window, flanked by dark painted jalousies fixed into the wall for continual ventilation. Another typical feature is the inner doors (one of which can be seen) known as "blinds". These are very practical as they allow some privacy and yet allow the occupant to look over the top when necessary.

The next house is thought to be about forty years old. It is of a very simple design and shows the common form of a wooden upper story on a stone base. This house has three doors downstairs, each with a pair of inner doors ("blinds"). The ground floor is occupied by an electronic business.

The third house was built by Mr. Winsor, a contractor in about 1840, and consists of two apartments. It still belongs to the original family and their descendants. The house has many typical West Indian features. Upstairs the narrow balcony is decorated with unusually pretty arched fretwork above, whilst the wooden balustrade is of an interesting design. There are two centrally located glass doors, with sash windows on either side, each flanked by dark painted wooden wall jalousies in the traditional West Indian way. The end gables of the roof are trimmed with lacy white fretwork which cannot be seen in the above view. Downstairs the outer doors are very plain when closed, but have a paneled inner side, seen when open. The traditional inner doors have now been replaced with full doors inset with frosted glass.

It is very pleasant to see this charming house has survived almost unchanged and it promises to look even prettier when the expected re-painting is completed.

Beauty in Decay

Back St (West End) Kingstown
V M Child

The Eastern end of Back Street (near the Hospital) is graced by a number of well- proportioned, traditional Kingstown style houses, some with long arched arcades. This sketch shows them as they were in the mid 1950s. I suspect that most of them were built in the middle of the nineteenth century.

Unfortunately these once fine homes are now in a run down state, probably because the owners predict that at some future date they might be acquired for demolition to make extensions to the nearby Hospital. Hopefully readers will take the time to have a good look at this one time attractive and dignified section of Back Street (Grenville St.).

In the background rises Cemetery Hill with a zigzag wall running uphill.

Grenville Street (Back Street)
Buildings in Real Kingstown Style

Here is a most attractive part of the city, as it exists at present. My hope is that people will read and notice these classical Vincentian style buildings with their cool arcades and appreciate them as part of our cultural heritage. In the foreground is the arcade of "Reesbank", a white washed brick and stone building that was the Connell family home. Some years ago it was rented to the S.P Bookshop, which supplied many schools and other books to the public.

Later Mrs. Antrobus opened the first boutique, "La Boutique", in Kingstown and much later, it was occupied by Eustace Auto Supplies. That business has now been transferred to another

51

beautiful Kingstown style house in Bay Street, which the owners have successfully renovated and improved.

Looking east down the pavement through the arches, one can see another example of this characteristic style. This is now the Anglican Cathedral Office. It is built of neatly dressed unpainted stonework, trimmed with usual brickwork around windows, arches and corner quoins. It has sash windows upstairs and an arched gallery sheltering the pavement beneath. It was probably built in the last half of the nineteenth century.

This house used to belong to the Rev. Flintoff. Rumour has it that he was a Roman Catholic priest who converted to become an Anglican priest in order to marry. He then had two daughters. An unmarried daughter inherited the house where she operated a little school for boys.

When Miss Flintoff became ill at the age of fifty-nine in 1931, she arranged with the Anglican Bishops to be supported by the Church for her remaining years in return for which the house would become the Church's property after her death. Despite remaining an invalid, who it is said never again left the house, she was not actually bedridden and unexpectedly survived for forty more years! She died in 1971 at the ripe old age of ninety-nine.

Changes in a House and the Co-Cathedral

The first sketch shows the house known as "Reesbank" as it was in the early years of this century. The house has a wooden upstairs gallery with five, shuttered casement windows supported by four

stout, tapered stone pillars. The second sketch shows the same house as it is now with a stone upper gallery with four sash windows supported by three beautiful arches.

This house is at least one hundred and twenty years old. I have been unable to discover the original builder, although it was probably Mr. Rees, as it appears to bear his name. In another respect this name is appropriate because the word, "Rees" is said to mean a stream in Gaelic and the North River does run beside the house. In 1915 Katherine, wife of Mr. Syble Boyle Cowley Connell, inherited this house from Mr. Rees.

In the 1930s, the upstairs wooden gallery had become rotten and it was necessary to replace it with a stone gallery. At that time, building techniques did not allow such a heavy structure to be supported by the four stone pillars. The builder insisted that the pillars be replaced by arches. While Mrs. Connell and some of the family were unhappy about losing the handsome pillars, the result is a most elegant home in the classic Kingstown architectural tradition of an arched arcade with four Georgian type sash windows above.

The arches in this house are particularly pleasing, because the upper parts are a complete semicircle. I mention this because for structural reasons, many of the arches of Kingstown arcades are flattened arches.

You will notice that the old house has a shingled roof, which was the usual roofing before the most economical and trouble free galvanised metal roofing became the normal roofing material of Kingstown. The sketch is taken from an old photograph very kindly lent to me by Miss Ruby Nanton.

Behind the house, the tower of the Roman Catholic Co-Cathedral, as well as the decorative Presbytery Tower built by Father Charles Verbecke can be seen. The former tower was shorter and wider. Father Charles Verbecke, who came to St. Vincent in 1919, renovated this building and he is responsible for the taller more slender tower. It is said that it was modelled after a church in Belgium and that the tower was too tall and had to be shortened, for safety reasons.

54

"The Playpen" and two Houses in Kingstown's Own Classic Style

The Western end of Grenville St. used to be purely residential and even now it is very peaceful except for motor traffic rushing through. For artistic effect (in this sketch) far more people than one usually sees have been put into the galleries under these houses, which are obliquely opposite the old Connell residence and the road by the Roman Catholic Cathedral.

The smaller house on the left has a traditional arched gallery, but the roof arrangement is unusual for Kingstown. It was owned for many years by the late O. D. Brisbane a merchant, well known not only in St. Vincent but also in several other West Indian islands. Bobbie Brisbane inherited it and sold it some years ago to a Mrs. Maskell.

Fortunately this pleasant looking house has recently been renovated and given a badly needed coat of paint. Even the window frames have been remade and happily the traditional sash type has been retained, the only difference being that they are now eight-pane, instead of the more conventional twelve pane windows. As the frontage of the building is rather small this has not altered its character.

The reason for all this work is that a new children's' Day Care Centre was opened within its walls. The centre was called "The Playpen" and it was run by the Hon. Speaker's wife, a trained nurse, Mrs. Douglas Williams. Beneath its cheerful white paint, the neat oblong stones, with lines of raised putty in between can clearly be seen, as can the bricks around the upper part of the arches.

The larger building, which belongs to Mrs. Douglas, is also built of neat stone blocks painted cream but with smooth putty between. It used to belong to the McDowall family, although they were not the original owners. Mr. McDowall was a merchant who raised seven children in this spacious home, which has a garden at the rear. After his death about fifty years ago, three of his daughters continued to live there. One of them became Mrs. Edwards, mother of Trevor and Clifford, both well known in musical and theatrical circles.

Pearl and Stacey continued to live in the residence. Stacey worked in Coreas Accounts Department. After Pearl's death she sold it to Mrs. Douglas.

The well-proportioned house has arches below of an unusual shape, supported by decorative pillars. The four front windows upstairs are of traditional sash type and are distinguished by unusually attractive green metal window hoods. The drawing does not do them justice and they are well deserving of a closer inspection. The hoods probably date from the early nineteen hundreds, although the house itself dates from the previous century. The present owner extols the way that these hoods have protected the window frames from the ravages of the sun and rain.

The next house painted a delicate shade of rose is very simple and has no gallery. It has been modernised unobtrusively.

An Unusual Belfry

The pretty little belfry adjoining the Kingstown Methodist Church may have gone unnoticed by many people. It was erected in 1907 and the sketch shows a rather unusual view of it from Middle St. which includes a corner of the main Methodist Church, constructed of gray brick with elegant white corner quoins and windows surrounds. It also includes St. George's Anglican Cathedral, the Prescod residence and other buildings in Higginson St. which is an interesting little street ascending a slope from Bay St. up to Back Street (Grenville St.).

The Methodist Church has existed for almost two hundred years in St. Vincent. It was in January 1787 that the first St. Vincent Methodist service was held. Everybody will remember what an important part the Methodist Church played in championing and educating the working masses in slavery times despite opposition from the "Establishment" of that period.

A few years after Emancipation, the present Kingstown Methodist Church, a fine massive rectangular building with a front of gray stone, and side and back of gray brick, with most attractive and distinctive diamond paned windows, was opened in 1841. Those who followed Sir Rupert John's interesting series of articles in THE VINCENTIAN on the "Methodist heritage" will remember the many "ups and downs" that have marked the previous and subsequent history of this fine church.

Congratulations to Eustace Auto Supplies Ltd…..

1984   Decaying

This elegant house built in the Kingstown classic style stands on the "Leeward" end of Bay St. It has an arched gallery below and well-proportioned Georgian type sash windows above. The construction of the front part is of stone with possibly some brick beneath plaster and whitewash. The back part used to have a gray tile hung wooden upper story. The house was in a very poor condition and was deteriorating, similar to many of the older houses at that end of town. It was likely built between 1820 and 1845 and used to belong to a Mr. Walker.

Eustace Auto Supplies Ltd. rescued it and did extensive renovations. The beautiful front part has been left intact with its arched gallery below and renovated sash windows above. Under the gallery the uninteresting and plain old wooden doors have been replaced with a very handsome arrangement of glass and aluminum large shop doors and windows. The decaying back part of the building has been rebuilt in concrete and new windows, which although not actually the classic sash, are pleasant for their position and have decorative window bars.

The forbidding high brick wall covered with decaying peeling old plaster to the side of the house has been pulled down and replaced with a most attractive decorative ironwork fence surmounting a low wall.

Attractive ironwork gates give entry into the spacious yard, which now has a large neat green overhanging shed. Everything else has been painted in shining white and the whole effect is most attractive and dignified.

As an interested observer of the city of Kingstown and its distinctive architecture, I congratulate this firm on this sensitive and improved reconstruction.

The Versatile Verbecke and his Marvellous Madonna Tower

In 1918 a Belgian monk and priest, Dom Charles Verbecke, left the Monastery of St. Benedict in Trinidad for St. Vincent, where he could enjoy greater independence to indulge his many talents.

Organist, linguist and architect, he set out to completely renovate St. Mary's Presbytery, a plain square building, built in 1891 through the energy of Father Collins.

Father Verbecke had a special machine and his own moulds to make small concrete blocks resembling bricks in colour and shape. He trained Vincentians to undertake the transformation of the Presbytery into a fantastic, beautifully crafted structure shown on the right of the sketch, with little courtyards and gardens with stone edged flowerbeds between the buildings and the rushing river.

It is a harmonious blend of Belgian, Venetian, and Romanesque architectural styles. There are elaborate curved upstairs galleries with very delicate arches. Father Verbecke's own sculptured face can be seen presiding over one of the courtyards between the Church and Presbytery. The splendid Madonna tower soars above the latter. Square airy arcaded tiers with graceful slender pillars support overlapping arches, flanked by corner pinnacles, surmounted by a crown like structure. It was built between 1923 and

1932, irrespective of some misleading tourist guide that claim that it must be much older. It was fortunate that Father Verbecke was helped financially by his family, owners of the Verbecke Publishing House in Belgium.

The St. Mary Presbytery's Madonna tower used to be about thirty feet taller because Father Verbecke had first built it with a pointed central pinnacle, which was damaged by an earthquake in the 1930s and had to be completely removed.

He also renovated the Church of Our Lady of the Assumption next door and the facade of the adjacent school, but they remained simpler buildings.

The original Roman Catholic Church in Kingstown used to be on the site now occupied by the Methodist Church. After being destroyed by a fire, the property was acquired by the Methodists, where in 1841 they built their own handsome church. When the Roman Catholics were ready to rebuild they had to do so on the long narrow strip of land between the North River and the road, during the last half of the nineteenth century. It was destroyed by a hurricane and rebuilt in 1875 from a design founded on one of the domestic chapels of the Pope in the Vatican.

Father Eardley erected a steeple in 1877. However, in 1898 another hurricane removed the pyramid on the top of the steeple. This was replaced by another wooden pyramid, which was removed by a gale in 1921. By that time Father Verbecke had arrived in St. Vincent and replaced the steeple by a wider top to the Church tower, which was completed in the 1930s. The church is now the Co-Cathedral of the Assumption.

Father Verbecke designed a beautiful house in Kingstown Park for priests. The energetic Father Verbecke did not confine his architectural talents to Kingstown. The much admired and elaborately built little church on the hill above Argyle was built by him to serve the then wattle and daub houses of the village of Escape, which housed cane cutters. Many years ago when cane was no longer grown there, the villagers moved and this lovely building was left stranded in its romantic situation on a hillside above the rough Argyle coast. Fortunately, in recent years it has become useful again as a school building.

This creative man was also responsible for the pretty R. C. Church at Rillan Hill and also churches in Mayreau and Canouan. I am assured that he also built the R. C. Church at Georgetown but its utilitarian simplicity is out of character unless it was much altered. In front of the old Cane Hall Estate House there were three large beautifully carved arches, which were designed by Verbecke. Unfortunately they remained separated from the front of the house because the plan to make them part of a front gallery never materialised. They have since been demolished.

Undoubtedly this imaginative man has left Kingstown and St. Vincent and the Grenadines enriched with very special buildings, the crowning glory being his lovely Madonna Tower.

St. George's Cathedral

In my research, I have concentrated mainly on buildings that do not get their fair share of appreciation or attention, however, for completeness there is a need to include the best known and admired buildings of the city.

This drawing of St. George's Anglican Cathedral shows its considerable length in a way seldom fully seen in a photograph.

The earliest Anglican Church was opened in 1720 but was destroyed in a hurricane 60 years later. The present edifice was opened in 1820, having been built of brick, with stone quoins and window surrounds, at a cost of 47,000 pounds, (a very considerable sum in those days), of which the Government had contributed 5,000 pounds. Unfortunately it cannot have been very well built, as early on considerable structural damage required expensive repairs.

A cupola surmounted the tower as is clearly seen in old prints of Kingstown. This was blown down in 1898 and while it was not replaced the top of the tower was embellished by the "battlements", which can be seen to this day.

To the right of the sketch one can see an addition of unpainted stone. These are the chancel and transepts, added between 1880 and 1887. This part of the Cathedral is built in a completely different style from the rest and has some beautiful stained glass windows best observed from within. One of these shows the women at the empty tomb, after Jesus Christ's resurrection, being addressed by a magnificent angel dressed in brilliant red. Underneath is written that it is in memory of the Duke of Clarence, one of Queen Victoria's sons who died in 1892. The Queen for whom it was made, felt that the angel should be robed in white, not red, and refused to keep it, thus it became a welcome addition to St. George's Cathedral.

It is worth walking round the outside of this stone addition to see the beautiful group of pointed windows that rise up at the east end behind the altar that stands within, and also to notice the charming curved vestry on the north side.

While not shown in the sketch, the Cathedral is surrounded by a large lush churchyard, which contains beautiful ornamental plants and trees, as well as gravestones and monuments. Railings and walls surround it and a wide straight path leads from the gates up to the pillared portico that is ideal for formal processions of all sorts. The path used to be shaded by an avenue of West Indian Almond trees, but is now open to the sunshine.

At present the older part of the Cathedral and the tower are painted pale yellow, contrasting with the white stone quoins and window surrounds. A few years ago it was painted pale blue.

The church became the Cathedral of the Diocese of the Windward Islands in 1877, when the Diocese shared a bishop with Barbados. In 1927 the Diocese acquired its own bishop, Alfred P. Berkley followed by Bishops Jackson and Tonks. They all held the post of Rector as well as Bishop, but in 1948 the Rev. Roland Stanley Maxwell became Rector.

This Cathedral has a beautiful interior with graceful airy upstairs galleries, which are often filled to capacity. There is a beautiful pulpit and a magnificent metal chandelier in the nave. The chancel and transept add great beauty to the most sacred east end. In

2002 the Cathedral acquired what is said to be the best organ in the Caribbean!

A Classic House

S. COMPANY

GRENVILLE St. 1986

V M Child

The Sprott residence, in poor condition at the time of writing, which stands on the Southside of Grenville St., was one of the finest examples of Kingstown style architecture. It is said to be one of the first residential buildings to be constructed in that part of town. It was the home of Mr. James Ellio Sprott born 1871. He moved there around 1905. It is thought that he may have built it himself, thus its age is at least 100 years old. The house has beautifully whitewashed plastered arches, which shelter the wide pavement of large flat flagstones. The upper story of this house is all wood and the outside is clad with white painted shingles. There are five elegant sash windows.

Within, the house has a beautiful wooden staircase leading to the upstairs with its ornate, airy woodcarvings, which fill the space between the tops of the wooden room partitions and the lofty ceilings.

Mr. J. E. Sprott was founder owner and Editor of St. Vincent's leading newspaper, "The Sentry" which later became "The Vincentian."

Sprott was an eminent man, who not only became senior member of the Legislative Council and also the Executive Council, which formed the Government of those days, but was also Chairman of the Kingstown Town Board. He died in 1925, at the age of fifty-four. His family all made significant contributions to the nation. Mrs. Sprott M. B. E. was active in many charitable organizations. She founded the Girl Guides in Kingstown and also the Anglican Soup Kitchen, which fed many poor elderly people from the building that is now the Anglican School on Bay St.

The eldest Sprott son was Louis who practiced as a Dental surgeon, followed by Vin, a civil servant and at one time a public relations officer who planned and made the early broadcasts on Radio St. Vincent back in the 1950s. Another project he undertook for the government was the formation of the Marketing Corporation to help growers market their produce. He was also Commissioner for the Boy Scouts of St. Vincent for many years. Vin was an accomplished pianist much in demand at social gatherings, and he was at the keyboard in Mariners Inn in 1977 when he collapsed with a severe stroke from which he died three days later. He was always cheerful and very kind as well as good company and has been sorely missed.

The third son, Jex also led an active life until his retirement from Hazells where at one time he held the position of Managing Director.

Nellie, his sister worked for many years in the Post Office and finally managing it, but in those days (1960s) of sex inequality, she was appointed only as Acting Postmaster. She was a very lively creative person who among other things composed a special amusing song for Princess Margaret on one of her visits.

Mabel, her sister was also a civil servant and at one time had the function of welcoming visitors at the wharf as well as the airports at Villa and the tiny old airport at Arnos Vale. She used to present each visitor with a rum punch. Mabel also started the St. Vincent Cubs, which she ran for many years.

While the Sprott house remains in very poor condition, the building to the left was renovated by Mr. Alves in 1981. He added an overhanging gallery, supported by two wide arches. There are two small houses on the right side of the Sprott residence.

We next have the Methodist Primary School. The side of the fine large Methodist Church constructed of dark gray brick can be seen on the right, but around the turn of the century the impressive Methodist Church Hall was erected, and has been in use for many events.

The Renovation of a Classic House

The Demarara Mutual management has kindly permitted me to use this lovely representation of their new premises from their 1987 calendar. The original drawing, made by Philmore John, provided the basis for John Crichton's screen print.

Formerly known as the Cropper house, this structure in classic Kingstown style, is built sturdily of neatly cut stone. As is usual in such houses, bricks surround the Georgian type windows, the three perfectly shaped arches that support the stone upstairs gallery and the corner quoins. The stone and brick walls are unpainted.

Unlike the renovation of some other buildings, carried out one or two decades ago in the city, a successful effort has been made to preserve the traditional character of this old house. Previously, renovations usually changed the windows so much in size and style that the special character of an old building was completely altered. Happily this happens less often at present. Traditionally shaped sash windows are now available with metal glazing bars to replace the old ones with their perishable old wooden glazing bars. Unfortunately however, these came with a black finish. Despite the glistening new glass and excellent proportions these new windows give a rather sombre impression when set in walls of grey brown stone. Traditionally we are accustomed to seeing window bars painted in cheerful friendly white, which contrasts pleasantly with the colour of the walls.

At the present time it is easy to see the different effects, by looking at the nearby "Kentucky Fried Chicken" building where some of the new sash window bars are black and some are white. The "Kentucky" building, formerly the "Fishnet" is in a similar style but is much larger and has recently been sensitively renovated by the new owner Ken Boyea, and his architect, Mario Spinella.

I have not been able to confirm the year in which the Demerara Mutual Building was constructed. Since some older people remember seeing it all their lives it must have been built before the end of the nineteenth century. Strangely very similar buildings are known to have been built in the nineteen thirties (e.g. the Cambridge House opposite the Government buildings in the Halifax section of Back Street), which shows the confidence and satisfaction felt by citizens in this practical and dignified Kingstown style, which gives a unique character to this little city.

Nathaniel Bassnet Cropper, owner of a drugstore elsewhere in town, raised his family here. It included four daughters, the eldest of whom was a noted local artist. Popular and well respected by all, until well into their nineties, the last of the Miss Croppers died in 1975.

Hillside Home Close to the Court House and White Chapel

This is a very charming and well-maintained hillside house, close to the Court House and White chapel. It has a stone lower story and the upper story is of wood. It is trimmed with decorative, white fretwork and the balcony rail is carved in an intricate lacy design. There are long windows opening onto the balcony and traditional sash windows at the sides. The lower side windows have wooden louvered shutters.

This house was built in the 1930s for Mr. Joseph Matthews, a civil servant. His son was Rudy Matthews, a chief engineer in the Public Works Department. The house has changed hands several times and now belongs to Mr. St. Clair Dacon. In the lower story is a most elegant hairdressing salon and over it is Mr. Dacon's office.

The upstairs rooms are divided by wooden partitions, which support lovely ornate openwork carvings that extend to the ceiling, allowing air to circulate freely. This attractive feature can still be admired in many Vincentian homes built before the age of the electric fan. It is interesting to note that this house was built as late as the 1930s in such an attractive traditional style, apparent both inside and out.

Next door can be seen a typical example of a very simple old Kingstown house with a single tile hung upper story with four hooded sash windows and a stone lower story with two doors. Many similar houses may still be seen in the city.

The "Fishnet" A Fine Example of Vincentian Town Architecture

This sketch depicts the handsome building known for the past few years as the "Fishnet". It is a fine example of Vincentian town architecture. It stands on a corner and its arches continue around that corner. It is constructed of brownish gray dressed stone, with brick work around the windows, the arches and the corners.

At the time this sketch was made the insides of the arches were whitewashed from top to bottom, which contrasted pleasantly with the darker stone and brick work. The building used to belong to the Joseph's who ran a drygoods store below and lived above. Later it belonged to Mr. Adams who created its beautiful garden with fountain in the inner courtyard and popular "Fishnet" restaurant above. It was in this building that the well-known firm of Campbell's Travel had its first office. There is now a new owner who is undertaking a sensitive renovation and an architect planned roof extension.

In the background can be seen the house where J. Bee's restaurant is situated with its lovely hanging greenery. At the time of this sketch, the exterior was plastered and painted in a light colour which has since been removed to show the mellow brickwork beneath. You will notice that there were three graceful arches. Unfortunately a truck ran into them and smashed them up a few years ago. It was then probably more economical to replace them with the three straight pillars.

In the roof is a very pretty dormer window seen best from the opposite side of the street. I have included a detail of it in the corner of the sketch. It is no longer the same.

Three Houses in Back Street

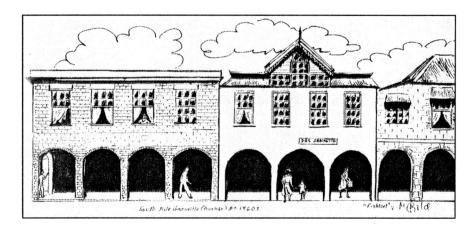

The first sketch shows three houses constructed in Kingstown's very own classic style. They have an arched arcade below and dignified sash windows above. The middle house also has a large decorative roof (dormer) window of a style sometimes seen in old houses of Georgetown, Guyana. Part of the large "Fishnet" building of stone, trimmed with brick, is seen on the right. The other two houses are built of brick, the middle one being painted a pale colour.

Big Apple

About 10 to 15 years ago "Big Apple", a well-known character returned to St. Vincent from the U.S.A. He was a big man with an outstanding personality and a lot of charm who can only be described as "larger than life"! It was no great surprise when he drove a great truck right into the elegant arches of the middle building, occupied at that time by "Das" Snackette. The result was that two of the old arches were completely destroyed and there was also structural damage to the upper story. This can be seen in the interesting photograph kindly lent to me by Mr. De Roche. "Big Apple" is said to have then returned to the U.S.A.

This accident necessitated extensive reconstruction, the results of which can be seen in the later picture. In 1985 the elaborate roof window was renovated in a more austere design. The house is now stripped to reveal a rosy brick construction. The gallery's simplicity is enhanced by green potted plants and hanging baskets.

The building to the left happily retains its downstairs gallery of flattered brick arches in front of Mr. Priddie's Horseshoe Restaurant, but there has been a complete change in the shape, form and numbers of the upstairs windows because of changes in the rooms upstairs which have been converted to offices.

Only a small part of the building on the right, once known as the "Fishnet" can be seen. Although the roof has been heightened to give extra accommodation, the well-proportioned sash windows have been given new frames. The lovely arched gallery below is as before. (This is a happy example of sensible modernisation).

Four Fine Houses and Three Tailors

These four attractive houses of typical Kingstown style, are mostly modified with modern window renovations. They adjoin the Bedford St. branch of the Barclays Bank and are in the Grenville St. end of Back St. opposite Sardine's Bakery.

The first house on the left was built of brick-trimmed stone in the 1920s, by the merchant and Estate owner Frederick Casson (formerly Corea). Later it belonged to the firm of Hadley Bros. who sold it to "The Royal Pharmacy" in the mid-seventies, where Mr. and Mrs. Kirby operate their popular drug store to this day. They let out offices above the three perfect arches that protect the pavement. The whole building is now painted in a cheerful shade of golden yellow and the roof is of green galvanize. The sash windows have been replaced with glass louver windows.

The second house is considerably wider than the others. It is also of stone with brick trimmings and it has three arches that are elongated and flattered to allow for extra width. The four upstairs windows have been replaced by smaller metal windows, due to the old window frames having rotted. The whole building is painted in an attractive shade of primrose yellow.

Tailoring has always been a most respected profession in St. Vincent. There were many more tailoring establishments in Kingstown about 40 to 50 years ago, because the prevailing fashion was for men to wear suits with jackets. Some men favoured suits all made of crisp white drill. Most of the tailors were very well dressed and even wore waistcoats at work!

In this house Mr. Messiah Eustace rented a portion of the ground floor for his tailoring business. This gentleman was noted for the immaculate way in which he personally dressed. He always wore a tailcoat when seen on the Street, which sometimes was white and sometimes other colours! He was the father of Mr. Roy Eustace.

The house was built around 1916 by Mr and Mrs. Joseph Burns Bonadie. The present owner is their granddaughter, Mrs. Ermine Williams, who still resides in the upstairs apartment. Her father was Mr. Alfred Clement de Bique, a well-known solicitor. When the 1935 riots broke out and the Administrator was attacked by a mob in the Courthouse yard nearby, he bravely rushed out to stop the violence. His efforts were bitterly resented by the rioters and his peacemaking attempt nearly brought him his death.

The third house belongs to the Jack family. It is the oldest of these four. In the early years of this century the wooden upstairs gallery, graced by five traditional sash windows with neat white window bars, was added on the front of an older building. Although the gallery joins its neighbours in projecting over the pavement, it is supported by four plain pillars presumably because wooden construction does not require the strength of arched supports. In the pre 2nd World War period in St. Vincent building regulations required arches to support heavy construction above.

The fourth house was also built by a tailor, Mr. Hilton Daisy and is still inhabited by his children and grandchildren. Another member of the family also runs a handicraft boutique. This is a handsome house of dressed stone, with brick trimming and two perfectly shaped arches below. It was built as late as 1936, in typical Kingstown style, after Mr. Daisy's smaller wooden one story house had to be demolished to halt the spread of a dangerous fire.

The galleries of these four houses together with others form a long and attractive arcade sheltering the pavement, which is thronged in working hours with busy people. The arcade continues almost uninterrupted to the fine,"Fishnet" building now carefully renovated and housing the "Kentucky Fried Chicken" restaurant at the corner of Melville St.

Traditional West Indian House

This picture shows a charming traditional West Indian house in a very prominent position such as might be seen in some of the other West Indian islands. When one is in the market area it looks very pretty. It was formerly painted pink and is now gray, against the dark green of the trees and lofty Mount. St. Andrew. The upper story is of wood on a stone or brick base. The sides are shingled and the wooden balcony from which one will have one of the busiest

75

views in town, has a green balustrade built before 1865, which was nearly destroyed by fire in 1979.

Mr. Hugh McConnie who headed the Agricultural Department a few years ago spent some of his childhood in this house. Mr. McConnie's Grandfather, Joseph Emmanuel Marshall, was an immigrant from Barbados who bought the house about 1865. He ran a shoemaking and shoe retail business on the ground floor. His daughter, Ada Marshall, continued the business.

In 1967 it was bought by the late Mr. Hinds and is now the property of his widow Mrs. Veda Hinds whose son ran a wholesale - retail grocery business on the ground floor. The upper story was a family dwelling. This building was demolished and the market woman seen in the sketch would now be inside the new market building.

The Heart of the Nation: The Courthouse
The site of many historic and ceremonial occasions

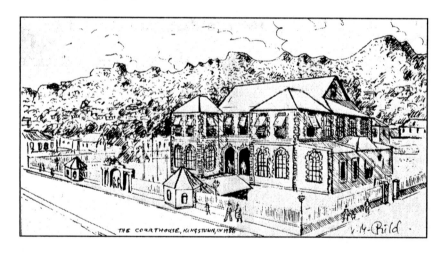

This handsome stone building stands in the middle of Kingstown. It dominates the Market Square, which lies on land that slopes gently down towards the sea. It is surrounded by a large grassy area within a white railing enclosure.

One enters through an arched stone gateway flanked by two narrower arched entrances. The railings are interrupted in two places by pretty little octagonal buildings with pointed red roofs. It is said that these were specially placed so that a good view could be obtained from the windows in all directions, of the whole length of Back Street. This was important when it was necessary to know the exact time of the Governor's arrival.

Not so long ago the enclosure contained several large shady trees making it a pleasant place for court witnesses and others to pass the time. As the trees aged and more parking spaces became necessary the trees were felled. The witnesses now have to wait in an open-sided shed, the roof of which can be seen in the above sketch.

On the other side of Back Street there were drinking troughs for horses, shaded by enormous old silk Cotton trees, which were felled during the first half of this century.

The Courthouse

The Courthouse itself is a fine old building made entirely of stone. Over the years several attempts have been made by officials to determine the age of the building, in response to enquiries from as far away as the British Houses of Parliament. Some have suggested that it must have been built at the same time as the prison building, which is a similar style and was constructed in 1872, although it was known that there was an earlier prison there.

Other evidence exists, however, to suggest that the Courthouse may in fact be much older. In the panoramic view of Kingstown shown in Caddy's print published in 1837, a building of very similar shape can be seen in the distance in the same position, above the market square which was then filled with many large trees. The windows in the gables appear fewer but this might be an error by the artist.

We know also, from Shepard's "Historical Account of the Island of St. Vincent" published in 1831, that
"The Courthouse is built of stone, and contains two rooms on the upper story appropriated for the sittings of the Council and Assembly, with two Committee Rooms below where the Courts of Justice are held. Here also are the public Offices of the Registrar and the Marshall. This building stands in front of the Market place, and is enclosed with an iron railing; behind it the Gaol..."

77

The building's wall is constructed of remarkably small and irregularly sized stones. This is in contrast to some of the typical Kingstown stone buildings of more than forty years ago where the stones have been carefully shaped into regular rectangles. The Courthouse does have, however, handsome neatly shaped stone corner quoins and window "surrounds". A few years ago they were picked out in pale cream or white paint, which made a striking contrast to the brownish grey stone of the walls. More recently they have been repainted in grey, which gives the whole structure a more sober appearance.

The actual courthouse is entered by passing through a small loggia of three lofty arches that befit the dignity of the proceedings that take place in the High Court of Justice. Above the gracious High Court is an enormous bright and lofty room lit by thirteen beautiful shaped large sash windows. It is here that the House of Assembly meets in surroundings of considerable dignity. The Magistrate Courts are also held here. The Registrar's office and several other such offices are also located in the Courthouse building.

So, the actual date of the initial construction remains a mystery; let's just say that the present style of the building could have been constructed at any time in the last two hundred years.

Whether the age of this impressive Courthouse is one hundred or so years or two hundred, or somewhere in between, the structure remains a fitting symbol of Justice and Democratic Government in the heart of the capital city of St. Vincent and the Grenadines.

"Iron Man" War Memorial

COURT HOUSE, SILK COTTON TREE

This picture is a photocopy of Mr. R.M. Anderson's photograph from the St. Vincent handbook, showing the "Iron Man" War Memorial and the Court House in the 1930s.

The big shady trees were enormous Silk Cotton trees in which nested many blackbirds whose droppings often besmirched the white cork hats of passing pedestrians. These hats were worn in those days as a protection against the feared effects of the tropical sun.

Around the time of the famous riots of the 1930s, there arose rumours that slaves may have been hung from these trees in the early 1800s. From what source these rumours sprang is unknown but evidently the crowd felt that someone must be punished. The Town Board, for emotional reasons I am told, but perhaps for more pragmatic reasons signed their death warrant and the massive trees were felled.

Thus this part of the Market Square, in which a fountain and trough for the many horses that brought people into town was situated, became devoid of cool shade.

In the 1960s Mr. Con De Freitas planted beautiful flowering vines, such as the orange flowered Macura and Thumbergias so both would run up and along a large trellis in order to provide beauty and also shade for those sitting on the handsome stone benches beneath.

Unfortunately authorities failed to prevent vandals repeatedly cutting the trunks of those vines until the Agricultural Department gave up. Only the benches and the trellis remain to this day. A Norfolk pine was planted near the "Iron Man". Although it is a native of the South Sea Islands, it gives an incongruous look to the centre of a tropical city. The pine provides no shade but it serves a good purpose as a decorated Christmas Tree.

"The Iron Man" is a fine statue of an ordinary humble man in uniform, erected in memory of those who gave their lives fighting for what in those periods of history appeared to be right. It was the defense of a reasonably ordered and comparatively free way of life, against the ruthless ambitions of military German Imperialism under the Kaiser and then under Hitler.

In the background of the picture, the Courthouse is visible.There used to be a variety of shade trees in the courtyard under which those summoned to court could wait in the cool shade. The Courthouse grounds are entered by a pretty gate and two charming little round buildings by the enclosed fence of iron railings. When the large new market building was erected, the Iron Man was moved to an even better site between the new building and Bay Street.

Two Typical Kingstown Houses and the Arrowroot Association

These two buildings, with typical arched arcades, are on the southeast end of Bay Street near the Grenadines wharf. Both belong to the Arrowroot Association. Unfortunately, the entire structure was demolished in 2004.

In the foreground is a very handsome stone building, which also used to be a private residence, erected it is thought by Mrs. Adie Agard who inherited it from her father, Mr. Linley, a retired sea captain. He owned considerable property in the vicinity, as well as being proprietor of Sharpes Estate.

The probable year of erection is 1912 though there is a possibility that it is an older building that was renovated. In front of the house was the beach with numerous small craft pulled under the shade of Flamboyant and Sandbox trees. Carpenters were usually busy building boats under those trees. Later the house is believed to have become a young people's social club. The walls are of neatly cut dressed stone with the customary brick quoins and window "surrounds".

The upstairs gallery is of stone and supported by thick arches with exceptionally stout pillars embellished with unusual horizontal decorative bands. Some people think that these pillars may have been reinforced when the Arrowroot Association used the building to house machinery as well as for storage of arrowroot.

The other building, which also has a long arched gallery was also a private residence at one time. The upper story has walls of unpainted galvanise probably put in by the Association to replace old wood. It was used for storage and the galvanise, which may be unattractive to the eye, but heats up in the sun and keeps the Arrowroot dry and free of moulds. The Association built two other buildings nearby, mostly of galvanise.

While the story of Arrowroot is currently discouraging, it was not always so. Mr. McDonald, a planter, was instrumental in putting the industry on its feet in the late 1920s and an agreement was formed among the planters, but unfortunately they did not all faithfully adhere to the price agreement. Mr. Casson (formerly Corea), a significant landowner and merchant, was influential in setting up the present association with the encouragement of Mr. George Mueller of the American starch merchant firm of Morningstar. The Government passed a bill and in 1930 the Arrowroot Association became the sole exporter of arrowroot. The industry was successful for many years and St. Vincent produced the purest known starch and enjoyed fame and a near monopoly.

It is unfortunate that these happy days did not last. The tragic collapse of the sugar industry at Mt. Bentinck back in 1962, was followed by an overproduction of arrowroot, causing an unmarketable glut. By the mid-sixties the Association had fallen into debt in order to meet its obligations to pay farmers for their starch. Banks withdrew credit. The British Government gave the St. Vincent Government (then in Crown Colony status), permission to guarantee farmers loans from the banks. The growers however, were to receive a much lower price for their produce. Production fell.

In the early 1970s conditions had improved considerably and stocks had been sold. Then it was discovered that there was a new use for arrowroot in the Computer Industry. An offer was made to buy sixty thousand barrels (200 lbs each) of arrowroot. Alas, St.

Vincent could, at that time offer only sixteen thousand barrels losing an excellent opportunity. The next set back was a fire at the San Souci factory in 1974.

In 1976 the Labour Government stepped in and repeated the original legislation by which the Association had been run by a majority of elected, mainly arrowroot growing members. They reduced the number of elected members in favour of an increased number of nominated members, with Government having authority to appoint the Chairman.

The recent history of the Arrowroot Association and Industry, of how the virtual monopoly and the major markets were lost, is well known to all interested persons and needs no repetition here, other than to sincerely hope that this industry, once the pride of St. Vincent, will soon revive.

The Public Works Building and a Bois Bois Man in 1910

This sketch is taken from a photo by vendor Proudfoot around 1910, depicting part of Back Street. On the right is the sturdy building now housing the Public Works Offices.

This building used to have a projecting wooden balcony that was later removed. A strange portion of this large building remains with exceptionally low arches (now flattered in shape) over the pavement. At one time the sidewalk (or pavement) beneath them was lower than the regular pavement, which caused a tall Chief Justice Harry O'Reilly to hit his head on one of the low arches as he ascended from the sunken part. He was so angry that he got the Town Board to immediately fill in this sunken pavement. At that time the house belonged to the Simmons family, but in 1928 Mr. H. A. Davis acquired it as a boarding house as well as his family residence. Beside the house was a garden with a fountain and a large swing seat and fruit trees. It is now a large parking area.

The public works building has recently had extensive renovation with the installation of smaller windows of a different design. In the street is a Bois Bois man. They used to parade in the streets of Kingstown and other towns at Carnival time and also at Christmas.

A well known practitioner of this dangerous stunt was Clarence Osborne who used to have his stilts tied on in the market square and then, dressed as a woman and sometimes wearing a frightening mask, he would strut in the streets to the accompaniment of a goat skin drum, shack shacks and flute. His head would be on a level with some of the upstairs windows of the town where he would appear to the occupants inside their upstairs sitting rooms.

Looking down the street there was a wall where there is now the small car park in front of Cable and Wireless. There was a residence and an old building where "Vinsure" now stands. Further beyond you can see one of the little round buildings near the courthouse.

The large trees that stood in the courthouse yard can be seen as well as the top of the large trees that stood opposite in the market square.

The small house on the left of the sketch used to belong to Mrs. Tina Thomas and later, after the second world war, it was acquired and rebuilt by Mr. Scott to house the Reliance Printery.

The Old Post Office

This sketch shows the building that is now the National Commercial Bank, as it used to be when it housed the Post Office, which was here for at least sixty years before it moved to more spacious premises beneath the new Government building at the beginning of the 1970s. The interior was very lofty and light with a very high ceiling, and in later years there was a glassed in office high up, from which the senior staff could survey all the happenings below.

In 1977 after extensive renovations and a complete internal change the building became the National Commercial Bank.

Postal history began in St. Vincent when Abraham Shaw was commissioned as the first postmaster. He, however, resided in Grenada and was also in charge of the Dominica and St. Lucia Postal Services. His successor, Middleton, was discharged for embezzlement.

It was not until 1778 that St. Vincent had its very own resident Postmaster, Daniel MacDowall, with a salary of 50 pounds per annum plus house rent and stationery. However, after only one year the French took possession of the island for four years, although it is probable that he would have remained in his job during that time.

Letters used to be sent out of St. Vincent by two main ways. "Ship Letters" were sent by private ship because the service was better and cheaper than the alternative Government packets, which between 1763 and 1778 hardly ever stopped at St. Vincent. Warships also carried mail.

After 1783 when St. Vincent was restored to British rule the "Jamaica Packet" sailed from "Falmouth", Jamaica, twice a month calling at Barbados, St. Vincent and Grenada. However, as with so many promising shipping arrangements even to this day, problems arose and there were fewer and fewer stops in St. Vincent. As a result a service of small schooners, called mail boats, started to transfer the mail to and from Barbados twice monthly for onward posting.

A Post Office is known to have been active in St. Vincent in 1783. In 1860 the control of West Indian Post Offices was transferred to local authorities, after which time British stamps were no longer technically permitted for use on the island.

In the same year (1860) former Jailer Robert Dalzell was appointed Colonial Postmaster of St. Vincent at a salary of 120 pounds per annum, plus a few small fees. He was also appointed Deputy Provost Marshall and in 1862, Bailiff of Fort Charlotte where he resided and received an additional salary of 35 pounds plus some rents. Unfortunately Dalzell, having many children to support, found himself in financial difficulties and 200 pounds was misappropriated, so he was suspended despite various appeals on his behalf. Nevertheless, in 1867, he was appointed Police Magistrate to the Grenadines.

In 1866 there was a fire in the Post Office and many letters were destroyed. The Post Office was at that time in the "Ordinance Building" said to be nearly opposite Mr. Nanton's Office" according to Pierre, Messenger and Lowe's Book, "St. Vincent" which deals with postal affairs and stamps of the island. It is not clear where that was but there is a photograph taken by Proudfoot around the turn of the century showing the post office to be in the building which is now the Electoral office, but used to be the Department of Tourism and previously the Surveys Department. It is still to be seen to the left of the flight of steps that leads up to the Government offices. To approach it one must now walk among the parked cars underneath the large new construction recently built in front of the old Government Offices and now the home of the Department of Tourism.

It is not known when the building in the drawing was constructed, but until its move in the early 1970s it was the home of the Post Office.

Once the Governor's Residence

This sketch shows the elegant old Government Office (still in use as such), built in classic Georgian style. This was before it was hidden. The small building to the left of the picture was the General Post Office at the turn of the century. It has since become the premises for many Government activities in succession, including the surveys Department, the Department of Tourism and the Electoral office. A modern upper story was added in recent years.

The Government offices building had been for many years clad in a thick coat of pale coloured wash (cream, if I remember rightly). A few years ago the walls were stripped and the beautiful, rosy coloured brickwork beneath was revealed. The simple central keystone-like decoration and wooden surrounds of each of the elegant sash windows were picked out in gleaming white paint, as was the large wooden porch to the front door above its imposing flight of steps. The lowest story has walls constructed, not of brick but rows of rough stone.

Soon after this attractive face-lift, a new set of offices was put on to the front of the building supported by utilitarian style pillars, stranding the small car park and the front steps. The Department of Tourism was moved into these spacious offices, which now obscure the view shown in the sketch.

The style of the building with its harmonious proportions is consistent with an age of at least two hundred years. However, I have not been able to ascertain the actual age and in St. Vincent, old styles have been used at much later dates (the old Public Library for example which is less than a hundred years old).

The large old building is almost square in shape, with five windows on each side of the upper floor. The back of the building remains complete in its restored beauty with another porch and a double flight of steps.

This elegance however, is now only to be seen from the car park behind the new Post Office and Ministerial Building, which now stand on the site of former tennis courts and a large Mango tree. Beyond them stood the lovely old Barclays Bank on the site of the present bank car park, beside which was an enchanting garden extending to the steep banks of the small river. The present Barclays Bank stands where that garden was.

There is a theory that this handsome building was once the Governor's official residence above the Government offices, probably then confined to the lower stone ground floor. Adding credibility to this theory are traces of great elegance inside the rooms of the middle and top stories. Probably the Governor had a retreat in the nearby coolness of the hill above the Botanic Gardens, which later developed into the so called Dasent Cottage and later with many additions around the end of the last century, formed the present Government House. This would be a very natural thing as the island developed and the ever-increasing need of Government for more and more office space encroached on the middle and upper floors of this handsome edifice.

An Interesting Renovation and a Classic House in Halifax Street

Restored Hadaway Building 1987
Cambridge Building in 1987.
J. M. Child.

The building on the left of the sketch is about one hundred years old but has been renovated more than once. Not long ago it was a typical Kingstown style house with four sash windows above three beautifully shaped arches below. It resembled the house next door. When extensive repairs were needed in 1983-84, the appearance changed drastically. The sash windows were replaced with metal casements and just three supporting pillars took the place of the three graceful arches despite all the owner's protests.

In December 1986 a vehicle crashed into the central pillar fracturing it to require structural repairs. Miss Clarice Hadaway, the owner then took the opportunity of reconstructing the arches. For practical reasons, however, two wide arches have been built instead of the original three.

Admirers of Kingstown's distinctive arcaded architecture must appreciate this effort to beautify Halifax St. with more arches. The house was originally built of blocks of concrete mixed with stone and it had been clad in a coat of beautiful, irregular cut stones, in a style that has now become most appreciated here in recent years, showing off the work of local masons with our beautiful local stone. An airy high upper story has replaced the old sloping galvanised roof.

The house next door is a perfect example of the untouched classic Kingstown style. It belongs to the Cambridge family. Upstairs are three dignified sash windows with hoods.

Interesting Mixture of Styles

The houses opposite the government buildings show an interesting mixture of styles on Back Street.

This sketch shows the buildings adjoining the "Bounty" opposite the Barclays Bank, and the Post Office and Government buildings in the grounds of the old Tennis Club. Apart from the "Bounty" it seems that there have only been two buildings of the old classic Kingstown style with arched arcades below. One of them can be seen on the right. It is a most perfect example built of neatly shaped gray stones with three beautifully proportioned arches below and three traditional sash windows, protected by window hoods above. This house belongs to Mr. Claude Cambridge. The house is almost the same as the Cropper house near the "Fishnet" building and the Cathedral Office both situated on other parts of Back St, (Grenville St. end).

The next house belonging to the Hadaways used to be similar but needed renovation and this was so thorough that the character has been completely changed. Although it was a most pleasant building it is sad that we have lost the characteristic arches, which are now replaced by three straight pillars, doubtless for important structural reasons. The building is occupied by the Venus Enterprises business and a boutique owned by Mr. Richards.

The next two houses were one-story structures for some time after they replaced old garages. The Reliance pharmacy was established in 1957 and was made into a two story building about fifteen years ago in the contemporary style used all over the Caribbean at that time. It is of a rather American type international style. An attractive feature is the decorative ceramic tiling of the lower part which is often seen in Portugal. A fine suite of offices was made available upstairs and the premises of this leading pharmacy were much enlarged.

The other building was built in 1946 by the "Val-U Electrical Service", and the upper story was added in 1957. Also in the contemporary style fashionable at that time, it has a ceramic tile facing on the ground floor. Both buildings are in harmony with surrounding buildings, in that they are of the same scale, which makes a good impression in a town street. (By that I mean windows and roofs are at about the same level.) The last building belongs to the Coombs family.

The architect is Mr. Trevor Thompson of Tomlin Voss & Co. The building is of a rather unusual non-traditional design. A very thick red-shingled roof projects from above the ground floor over part of the pavement. The purpose of the thick design, was to reflect the shape of some of the window hoods seen in the older buildings of

91

Kingstown. This building is also in scale harmony with the other nearby buildings. The building was constructed in 1982 by contractor Ken Minors, to replace a small old wooden house. At present Basil's Video Centre occupies the ground floor.

A Mystery Building

This charming building stands opposite Barclays Bank in Halifax St. The stonework is painted cream with the window hoods and lower part of the wall picked out in brilliant emerald green.

It is not known exactly when this building was constructed but it is at least one hundred years old. It is the only house built in this style in Kingstown and probably in the whole of the English and French speaking West Indies.

In England in the southwestern country of Devonshire there is a village called Topsham, built on the banks of the wide estuary of the river Exe. In the seventeenth century, Dutch refugees, fleeing from persecution in Holland, settled in Topsham and built streets of houses looking like the "Bounty."

I doubt if this type of house was seen elsewhere in England. The distinctive feature of these houses is that they have a flat side gable facing on to the street and the main entrance to the house is on the long side facing into a walled courtyard on the side. This is the shape of the "Bounty" building although, for business purposes, there is now an additional door that faces onto the street and the courtyard on the side has been roofed in. How it came about that this house of old Dutch style came to be built in the middle of Kingstown is a mystery.

At one time the house was the home of Mr. Smith (not Alexander Smith) and later it was sold to the Fraser family. It was often rented out as a residence. In the early fifties an Antiguan, Mr. Anjo started "The Snow White Ice Cream Parlour" where exceptionally delicious ice cream sundaes and banana splits with special toppings were served. The name must derive from the Snow White, heroine of the first full length cartoon produced in 1938 by the genius, the late Walt Disney called "Snow White and the Seven Dwarfs". This was also the first Walt Disney Cartoon to feature people instead of animals. Previously Walt Disney Cartoons had only animals such as Mickey Mouse and Donald Duck as principal characters. Seniors, and some not so senior, will remember the delight with which they viewed this animated fairy tale of a Princess and her wicked step Mother, with its beauty and songs as well as the always humourous seven dwarfs.

In the late 1950s Mr. Gibbons, an English engineering consultant travelled from India in response to an advertisement offering the Bequia estate of Amboise for sale. The estate was located in an area now occupied by the Friendship Bay Hotel. He was unable to purchase the property on the terms he had hoped and used his resources to acquire and run a business in the house featured here. He changed its name to the "Beachcomber" and its character to a popular café for light foods and drinks of all kinds. He installed bamboo partitions, which gave a measure of privacy to each little table.

The business was taken over by the Connell family who again changed its name and character. It became the "Bounty" and

93

received a ship like décor and an anchor across its street side. It was named "Bounty" after the famous ship of Captain Bligh who you will recall brought the breadfruit from the south-sea islands to St. Vincent in 1793.

Tourists will be quick to point out that the "Bounty" was Bligh's ship on his first successful attempt in 1789 to bring the breadfruit to the West Indies, but history tells us that the famous <u>mutiny</u> occurred on the "Bounty" and Captain Bligh was set adrift with other members of his crew. It was on his second attempt that he succeeded in bringing that beneficent tree to St.Vincent on board the "Providence" by means of suckers carefully nurtured on the long voyage.

The "Bounty" in Kingstown is now a most popular restaurant, providing light meals, snacks, ice creams and delicious home-made cakes. In a way it is also an informal cultural centre due to the many activities of the actor dancer, Tracey Connell, who can usually be found there in a supervisory role by day. Last but not least, paintings of local artists of St. Vincent are always on display and can be purchased at modest prices. (This restaurant has now moved to an upstairs location on Egmont Street.)

Barclay's celebrates 150 Years

It is quite possible that this was the original building for Barclay's bank when it was founded in 1837, although it might have been built any time in the last century.

The building was of mellow, reddish coloured brick construction, trimmed with regular courses of gray stone and handsome corner quoins also of gray stone, their edges intended in the "Buginato" manner. The windows were Georgian style sash windows, screened from the sun with push out slatted shutters painted green. I am told that this type of shutter is known as "Demarara". The manager used to live in a spacious apartment on the upper floor.

Note the dignified white porch and the elegant white gateway reminiscent of the courthouse gateway; also the spear design fence. One can only wonder what was the fate of that gateway, because an American expatriate called Mr. Sweeney, from whom the Prime Minister's official residence was purchased some years ago, made every possible attempt to purchase the lovely arched and pilaster decorated gateway structures to embellish the entrance to his large house.

He was frustrated in his attempt, which is a pity when one considers how suitable they would be now at the entrance to a house that has become such an important building. Even the iron gates are designed with singular grace. Note that "Colonial Bank" is carved over the lintel of the porch but when it became Barclays Bank DCO, (Dominion, Colonial and Overseas) a metal notice was attached to a gateway pillar. On the opposite pillar are the opening times, as they were in the 1950s; 9 to 2 everyday, including Saturdays, except Wednesdays when it closed at 12.

The old building was pulled down without as far as I know, any regrets or protests in the 1950s and replaced by the present one story building in what used to be a large and beautifully maintained garden that stretched between the old Bank building and the little river. It has since undergone alterations. The old building stood in what is now the Car Park. A new home was constructed for the Bank Manager up at Cane Garden where another, less public garden was created.

The Old Agricultural Exhibitions by Richmond Hill School

Many people will remember the popular Agricultural Exhibitions that used to be held every four years until suddenly cancelled, which must have disappointed many farmers and others preparing their animals and samples of their products, agricultural, industrial, artistic and craft work of all kinds. These exhibitions used to be held around the extensive school playing fields by the Richmond Hill School and Prep School. The exhibitions were started by the late Hugh McConnie, who was Chief Agricultural Officer at the time.

There used to be long row of neat booths hired by businesses of all kinds. Farm animals of all sorts were paraded and competed for prizes. There was always a beautiful display of fruits and vegetables impressively arranged on a long table upstairs in the Richmond Hill Schools. Downstairs there were displays of intricate and beautiful needlework etc. Lovely cakes and edibles were also on display. In the Prep School, works of art such as paintings by local artists were to be seen. Other products by local manufacturers such as plumbing fixtures were also shown.

"Reigate"

Some will remember that this site once contained the charming old house known as "Reigate" which you can see in the above photograph. It used to stand in a large well-kept garden with much lawn. No longer did this beautiful house stand in a place suitable for a quiet residence, because it was now in the middle of a busy part of the city. In 1988 it was renovated and the upstairs was used as a restaurant with some small shops below. Most of the large lawn had gone long before when the Baynes Building was constructed there.

This valuable site was purchased a few years ago by the NBC Bank and the house was demolished. It is nice to note that the very dense dark green tree in the front of the site still remains; I understand that it is a "Black Ebony".

97

We must look forward to seeing another beautiful building on this important site. Hopefully its style will not conflict with the elegance of the old Carnegie Library building opposite. There have been a number of attractive new buildings in Kingstown in very recent years, in contrast to the somewhat "brutalistic" so called "modern" style of the 60s, 70s and 80s, so I live in hope that the new buildings that will occupy this site will enhance the appearance of the city.

My sketch shows how "Reigate" used to be. It belonged to Mr. Jim Hazell, a nephew of J.H. Hazell who founded Hazell's, that was for many years one of the leading stores of Kingstown. In 1928 the house was sold to Mr. V. M. Verrol, an Englishman who worked at Hazell's and eventually became the manager. The house was probably built either at the end of the 19th century or the beginning of the 20th Mr. Percy Edwards was very helpful to Mr. Verrol in many ways and became devoted to the four Edwards sons, Trevor, Arthur, Gerald and Clifford who inherited the property.

One of the distinctive features of "Reigate" was the two flights of steps joining into one flight to reach the upper story decorated by a pretty shady gallery (or veranda). This type can still be seen in many Barbadian residences.

A Library of Single Elegance

The old Public Library, one of the most beautiful and well-proportioned buildings in Kingstown, stands in a prominent position in its beautiful triangle of lawn with gorgeous ornamental trees in the fork of the little South River.

The Library was built back in 1909 through the generosity of the American millionaire, Andrew Carnegie. This benefactor born in humble circumstances in Scotland in 1835, educated himself by the use of libraries and eventually made a fortune in America with iron and steel works. He died in 1919.

The library was built of dressed gray stone in a traditional late Georgian style with decorative parapets and plastered gables. The entrance is embellished by a lofty narrow two-pillared portico, with a balcony above. Two wide bow windows at each side of the building relieve its rather austere simplicity. It is these proportions that give it a lovely shape. There is a most attractive wooden staircase with carved banisters on both sides.

Like eyes in a face, the shape and placing of windows in any building is important for the whole character and appearance. The sash windows of the library are beautifully proportioned, tall and slender, crowned with little cornices and harmoniously placed in the walls.

99

In the 1950s the Library walls were of unpainted gray stone and looked quite well without benefit of paint or plaster (except on the decorated gables and parapet). When Princess Margaret visited St. Vincent in the days of Federation it was felt necessary to slap a coat of gleaming whitewash all over it in her honour. Unfortunately this meant the constant expense of repainting to keep the library from looking shabby.

These rough sketches only give a slight idea and omit many details. Please, dear readers, have a good look at the library and its charming details both without and within. Above all do not take its elegance for granted.

Towards the end of the last century, the library became dilapidated. Fortunately, the Alliance Francaise came to the rescue and in return acquired the use of the upper floor for educational purposes. Meanwhile the public library has moved to another location in the city.

Three Buildings Before Harbour Reclamation

This photo shows three buildings that remain the same as they were twenty or thirty years ago. The difference in the picture is that the harbour reclamation scheme (late 1960s) had not yet taken place and the beach is on one side of Bay St., thus the sea is very close. The building on the right is a small part of the old Public Library building.

Then comes a large corner of the Blue Caribbean building, which is built in classic Vincentian urban style, with sash windows and graceful hoods and with a long arched gallery below. At the time of the sketch it was the leading hotel of Kingstown. On the left of the picture behind the library garden, the back of the Heron Hotel with its pretty upstairs porch can be seen. At that time this hotel was South Bridge Hotel and before that it was a private house. Finally the pretty Library garden is a joy to the eye and remains so up to this day.

Some Special Trees

There is a row of very fine trees, each of a different variety near the banks of the little South River. The river runs under the pretty bridges beside the wide street that leaves Back St. (Halifax St. end) near the Library. This thoroughfare enters Bay St between the Blue Caribbean Building and the Heron Hotel.

On the right of the sketch is a graceful tree with large flowers of a delicate pale mauve shade and soft dropping leaves, Superficially it resembles a West Indian white cedar in flower. The truth is that Mr. Con DeFreitas planted it in the 1960s as an alleged purple Poui and he admits that it has not turned out quite as he intended. Nevertheless, it provides welcome shade under which a shining mobile metal booth provides popular hot snacks.

The next tree is a typical West Indian Almond tree with large tough glossy leaves which periodically turn red. This common variety of tree grows very fast and in distinctive flat layers of leaves. It was planted by taxi drivers to provide shade for their vehicles.

The next tree is a small Ebony adorning the vivid velvety green lawns of the public library. The Ebony grows wild in the drier parts of Jamaica and in season it is covered with small yellow flowers. It was planted by Mr. Con DeFreitas who was at one time Director of the Department of Agriculture. He remains an encyclopedic authority on the flora of St. Vincent and the Grenadines. Next is a lovely Flamboyant tree. Con tells me that he planted it as an alleged bearer of yellow blossoms instead of the more common scarlet. It turned out however, to bear more blooms of a rather unusual orange hue, which can be admired around July and August in contrast with the nearby purple and crimson Bougainvilleas. Even when not blooming the Flamboyant is a beautiful tree with its delicate feathery pale green foliage and long brown dependant seedpods. On the left is a tree that is very unusual in St. Vincent, The foliage is amazingly dense and dark and compact. It is a black Willow more often seen in other West Indian Islands.

This tree was planted by the late Mr. Verrol in the front yard of his charming old house on the North side of Back St opposite the Library. This house was demolished but the tree was preserved.

Changes in Granby Street

This sketch shows the east side of Granby Street as it looked in the 1950s. On the right is Granby House, an old white building constructed in old Kingstown style with a wooden upstairs gallery, supported by one arch and pillars over the pavement. It was probably built in the middle of the nineteenth century. At the time of the sketch, the house was occupied by three sisters, members of the Richards family who maintained a lovely small town garden. When they became older they moved to a new home in Barbados in the late 50s.

The next occupant was Emmanuel High School after their old premises in Victoria Park were burnt to the ground. The school remained there for about 15 years. In the early 1970s or thereabouts the firm of W.J. Abbott and Sons rented the Methodist Church and have used it as a storeroom to this day. The house remains as it was, except that the pavement part under the upstairs gallery has been blocked in.

The next house is Granby Cottage adjoined by Granby Lodge. These two charming houses were built by architect John George Nanton for Mr. Smith, a lawyer from Aberdeen who died in 1884. Both these men were great grandfathers of Mrs. Clara Layne (of Edwin Laynes & Sons Ltd.).

Granby Lodge was a particularly attractive classic Kingstown residence. It was painted in two shades of shell pink and the high, arched gallery was enclosed by a neat picket. A little wooden balcony projected over the pavement. Note the unusual design of the dormer window in the roof. The upper story had shingled walls. Mr. Smith's family and descendants lived in these houses and another one behind, until in later years they were rented to others.

Eventually they were dismantled in the late 1960s by the owners to make room for their new lumber yard. Recently the premises also house Layne's Hardware.

The last house in the sketch, with its gray shingled, upper story, was large and very dilapidated. It once belonged to a Sutherland family and was dismantled and replaced by a very useful McConnie Yammie Supermarket.

This once quiet residential street is now an important part of the commercial heart of the city.

An Elegant Renovation

When you walk or drive from the Customs and Port area up Sharpe
Street, you will notice this beautiful building on the corner of Middle
Street. This is an old house, built sometime in the second half of the
19th century and had no special distinction until its renovation by
Kenny Minors for Clara Layne was completed.

Notice the simple, but pleasing wooden louvered window in
the middle of the wide, white gable. The upper story had its plaster
removed to reveal brickwork of a particularly pleasing pinkish, red
colour. This is well shown off by the white paint on the corner
quoins, the gable, the window surrounds and the strip that divides the
upper story from the lower.

The walls of the ground floor have also been cleaned of
plaster and reveal a rather random stone work, which was unlikely to
have been planned for unplastered viewing, otherwise it would have
been very carefully cut into rectangular blocks, similar to the

"Fishnet" and other buildings. Nevertheless the effect is very attractive and is emphasized by the white painted door and window surrounds. The security gates and the window bars are of a criss-cross type of metal work, which also adds favourably to the overall general effect.

A Portuguese family called Neaves used to live in this home until the owner of Argyle Estate, Alexander Smith, the great uncle of Clara Layne, bought it from them in the late 1900s. It was probably built during the last half of that century.

Alexander Smith was the son of William Smith, who rebuilt at his own expense, the Scottish Kirk, (now the Seventh Day Adventist Church) after the 1898 hurricane. He kept the house unoccupied and bequeathed it to his nephew, William Nanton, who left it to Clara Layne (nee Nanton), wife of Edwin Layne (Edwin Layne & Sons Dry Goods Store).

She and her husband lived in the house with its spacious upstairs rooms and inner courtyard rose garden, but found the area too noisy. Since then it has been rented out periodically, but for the last 30 years or so has had a closed up, lifeless look.

My personal thanks to Keith Boyes for allowing me to use his excellent photo of the building taken by photographer Dale John, as a basis for this drawing.

A Sad Murder

This photo shows part of Granby Street as it was in the late 1950s. The church was rebuilt by William Smith in 1850 and was the Scottish Kirk for the Presbyterians of St. Vincent. Alexander Porter, a one time large landholder, endowed it sometime in the

early 1900s.

Unfortunately, they had an unsatisfactory minister for many years, during which the congregation dwindled.

The Rev. Wilson arrived to revive it and in the 1930s, the Rev. Mayne Stewart was sent from Scotland. Owing to her friendship with two elderly ladies of the congregation, a Roman Catholic, married lady used to help with Kirk functions. The husband of this lady arrived home one night and in a jealous rage shot a man dead. The man was not the minister he had intended to shoot, but his own brother! After this tragic scandal, the Rev. Mayne Stewart left and the church closed down. The endowment went back to the Porter family (according to one of the conditions of the original agreement), to help a nephew who was in bad circumstances in Barbados.

Happily, the Seventh Day Adventist Church acquired the building and renovated it without changing its attractive appearance.

In the sketch the residence of Mr. F. Thompson can be seen beside the church. it was an attractive example of West Indian Vernacular style. The upper story is of wood. At the time the sketch was made it had not yet been cruelly damaged by vandals. The pretty shape of the decorated gables can still be appreciated with the church gable and elegant tower rising up behind. It has since been replaced by a large modern building. In the distance can be seen the old building that used to be Velma Browne and Sons.

Sharpe Street

Some readers may be hard put to recognise the locality depicted by this sketch of Kingstown in the late 1950s. The street looks very clean and shows typical buildings and in the foreground a little arched gallery.

This gallery is under the building once occupied by the St. Vincent Banana Association. It has remained the same except for a change in the windows, which have been made much smaller, presumably because of the requirements of air conditioning. The window shown has now been completely blocked up.

The walls have a rather unusual finish common to a few of the older houses in Kingstown; they are plastered but grooves have been made in the plaster to make it look like neat stonework covered by wash. The building next to it had, at that time, a shingle hung upper story. On the other side of the street can be seen the building that is now Hillocks and much changed. It also had a shingle hung upper story. Next to it is the Hadaway Tailoring shop with wooden upper story. Beyond is the building that has now been completely modernised to make the popular Velma Browne and Sons store.

In the case the reader still does not recognise this street it is Sharpe Street that runs uphill from the dockside to Granby Street.

A Pretty House Near the Port

At the continuation of the Southern end of Bay Street, past the Arrowroot Association towards the old Harbour Club, one encounters several pretty houses. This enchanting white wooden house used to be very small and simple when first built around 1890.

Mr. Renald Lambert Eustace bought it from Mr. George Corea (self made businessman and estate owner). The charming gallery, decorated with diagonally patterned fretwork above and a pretty wooden balustrade below, was the work of a Trinidadian craftsman. At about the same time the enclosed gallery or living room overlooking the street was added with its own red galvanised gabled roof and three elegant sash windows separated by two dark

green fixed wooden louvers.

The house has a view of the Harbour below. It is surrounded by a small garden, full of beautiful plants and ferns behind a wall enhanced with a few rows of decorated blocks. The iron garden gate has a pretty scrollwork design.

Behind the house rises a steep hill thickly covered with trees concealing a number of small houses.

An Unfamiliar Look to a Familiar Corner and a Mysterious Fire that Caused a Famous School to Move

Only a small number of readers will immediately recognise this view. The sketch shows the Southern corner of Victoria Park before it was enclosed in the late fifties presumably in order to allow something to be to earned from the activities held within, such as sporting events and Carnival. By that time it was beginning to lose its former popularity as one of the most desirable residential areas as the move out to the suburbs was then becoming fashionable.

On the left is Park house, which belonged from 1919 to Claude Richards, the hard working owner of remote Petit Bordel Estate. Later it was sold to Ormond Nanton eventually deteriorating so badly that it was pulled down.

The next building, which has a front on one side of Back Street, was known as Tyrell House and it belonged to Nanton's parents. Formerly it belonged to the Simmons family and later it was sold to Alec Fraser. Probably these houses date from the middle of the 19th century. There were elegant carved pieces of lattice work above the room partitions. Neither building survived beyond the 1980s.

At one time Tyrell House was used for some of the classes of the Girls High School whose main building was located at the current site of the Public Health offices (on Back Street). From around 1947, Tyrell House and an adjacent building were rented to accommodate Dr. J.P. Eustace's Emmanuel High School. For many years this was the biggest Secondary School in the island, with about six hundred pupils, until July 1966 when sadly it burnt level to the ground under mysterious circumstances, All records were lost as well as the ground floor bookshop, with its valuable stock of school books maintained by Mrs. Eustace.

Houses by Victoria Park

Victoria Park, named after Queen Victoria was very much in our thoughts during the Independence celebrations presided over by her great-grand daughter, her majesty Queen Elizabeth and his Royal Highness, the Duke of Edinburgh.

This picture shows houses along the Western side as they were in the 1950s before the enclosure. The next house is also still unchanged and, in fact, is in better condition than before. The next house can no longer be seen, as the front yard has been built upon. Notice the unusually pretty white fretwork arches decorating the balcony. Next is the Freemasons Lodge, an attractive building that can be seen in 19th century pictures. It has been repainted in white, but the arched gallery on the ground floor has closed. Fortunately, an attempt was been made to preserve the graceful outline of the two arches, which had long ago been fenced in to prevent use of the gallery by pedestrians. The next building belongs to Miss Doreen Hadley and was built by Mr. Everard Richards or his brothers in the 1920s or 1930s, in a traditional simple style that could have fitted into an earlier period.

After an empty lot, the sketch shows an attractive old house that used to belong to the Hazell family, which was pulled down some years ago to make way for an Evangelical Church.

Next comes the oldest house of them all, which can be seen in old prints including Harrid's print of Kingstown published in 1837. The house was built in 1806 as officers quarters for the Military. It came into the possession of the Anglican Church some time before 1870 and was the residence of Rectors and sometimes Bishops until it became the official Bishop's residence in 1969, when our present Archbishop Woodroffe became Bishop of the Windward Islands.

At one time, Arch Deacon Maxwell (a physicist) used to live in that house. He was well-known as the author of the textbook, "Heat, Light and Sound" which was the text used when I was a "pre-med" student' knowing nothing of St. Vincent. This house is rather tall as were many of the older houses according to old prints. It has two elegant windows in the two gables known to architects as paladin windows. The house has recently undergone some internal alterations with great improvement.

In 1887 trees were planted by the Governor's wife, Mrs. Sendall and other ladies. It survives but is no longer the Bishop's Residence. The park was named Victoria Park in honour of Queen Victoria's sixtieth anniversary (or Jubilee) on the throne.

It is a beautiful name commemorating a great Queen. It would be a great pity for anyone to consider changing the name again as it would probably continue to be changed every few decades until all continuity of our historical heritage would be lost. There have been too many place names changed in St. Vincent and the Grenadines as anyone who has consulted old books will discover to his confusion and dismay.

113

It is difficult for readers to be sure as to what places the books refer as names get changed beyond recognition. There are always many new awards, new activities, new buildings, new institutions etc. that could be named to commemorate heroes or worthy citizens, thus leaving a heritage of continuity understandable to future generations.

Soaring Palms and Lovely Towers

This sketch shows the eastern side of Victoria Park before its enclosure in the mid fifties. On the other side of the lively little Kingstown North River, running hidden in its ravine, rise three beautiful towers from right to left; the Cathedral of the Assumption, the lacy tower of the St. Mary's Presbytery and St. George's Anglican Cathedral. At the edge of the park itself, eight graceful cabbage palms wave their graceful fronds high above everything else.

Opinions vary as to when they were planted. In the mid fifties there was a move to fell them on the plea that they interfered with the sporting activities on the park. Local protests happily averted this but very soon after, the park itself was enclosed except for the precipitous river boundary, which later also received a boundary wall in an attempt to keep out agile small boys and others when certain special events were in progress. Fortunately, the unsightly galvanized fence that surrounded the park for so many years was eventually replaced with an inoffensive wall of concrete blocks.

At the time of this picture there was just one small stand for spectators (not shown in this sketch) which still takes pride of place among the newer stands that were all filled to capacity for the Queen's most successful visit and our independence celebrations.

To return to the lovely Cabbage Palms, of which there were eight in the mid 1970s, there now remain only three and I am told on good authority that there is a plan to replant them all. One fell down harmlessly and two others had to be felled as they had become old and were in poor condition. It is to be hoped that the new ones will grow quickly as they make a striking and stately background to our ever-improving national events. In some old pictures of Kingstown, one can see similar palms waving all along the North side of Back Street and in other places such as Paul's Lot.

The square sturdy battlemented tower of St. George's Cathedral, rebuilt in 1820 is seen in the background among trees on the left.

As explained earlier, the Presbytery buildings were the imaginative work of a very popular Belgian Benedictine monk called Father Verbecke who rebuilt it after the original wooden structure was damaged in the 1921 hurricane. This beautiful brick and stone building was completed in the early thirties. With its balconies, arcades and small courtyard gardens it is a glorious blend of Spanish, Moorish and Venetian Gothic above which rises the elaborate but airy tower whose height is reminiscent of the high towers of public buildings in Belgian cities.

Then comes the tower of the Co-Cathedral of the Assumption rebuilt in 1875 after a hurricane. Father Eardley erected the steeple in 1877 but it was damaged by hurricanes in 1898 and 1921. Father Verbecke changed the steeple making it taller with a wide part at the top under the pyramid roof.

Wooden House on North Side of Victoria Park

This attractive wooden house, which is on the North side of Victoria Park, was built later than both of the adjacent Bishop's house and the old house nearby belonging to Miss K. Durrant. Mr. Kernahan was a Government surveyor of islands from Trinidad and he married a Vincentian, a sister of the Kings Counsel lawyer, Mr. Conrad Simmons. The house was built for them to start their married life around 1910, either by Mr. Kernahan or perhaps a gift from the bride's father, Mr. Charles Simmons.

In the 1920s Mr. Alban DosSantos of Colonarie bought it with ample land, for a sum equivalent to about E. C. $6000.00! This may seem astonishingly low until one hears that at that time rice sold at 1/2 to 1 cent per lb. according to quality. Mr. Dos Santos raised a large family, which made it necessary for him to make additions to the house.

For clarity, I have omitted the wooden and later concrete block fence, which surmounts the stone wall bounding the garden.

An unusual feature of this house is the bow window effect at both ends of the upstairs gallery. On the eastern side, which is not in the sketch, there are three bay windows projecting out, supported on narrow pillars.

The stone steps leading to the upstairs gallery and front door is a very West Indian feature seen in several other West Indian islands. Halfway down, the steps spread out in three directions with a graceful curve. Apart from decorating the front of a house, outside flights of stone steps were probably developed as a safety measure for escaping from wooden buildings in the case of fire. All over St. Vincent one can still see stone steps leading up to other houses. Overgrown with weeds and undergrowth, one can often find stone staircases surviving where the rest of a house has vanished (removed, burnt or decayed).

In the mid fifties the house was sold to the Anglican Church as a most desirable residence with its lovely view of the sea and Grenadines beyond the green expanse of the park with its few well-placed trees. The house was then called the 'Deanery'. A

few months after this, the park was enclosed and soon a large grandstand was erected, effectively terminating the beautiful view. Fortunately there are plans afoot to renovate this charming old house, which is now used as a centre for the elderly.

117

Precious Arcades, the Pride of the City

This is a picture of an arcade in Kingstown. I hope this sketch which has appeared earlier in the book, underscores how much more elegant, as well as more protective for pedestrians from the elements, are the arched arcades, especially when one can see the arches superimposed one over the other over a long length of pavement.

The arches are under the Sprott Residence, the Alves building and the Demarara Life building.

In most cases it seems that arches were constructed because of their superior strength to support upstairs galleries of brick or stone, which with the older local building methods could not be supported by widely placed simple straight pillars. The Sprott house is one of the few exceptions where arches support a gallery made only of wood.

There are many cities where pillars support storys over the pavement, but there are not many in the English or French speaking

Caribbean. The arched arcades of Kingstown are definitely a special feature of our city, and in my view should be carefully preserved, or replaced in the correct (if possible) proportions and kept well maintained. If that is done we can boast of a very special little capital city that we can be proud of with its own unique street architecture. The closest, somewhat similar but still different buildings and still a long way from St. Vincent, are found in Charlotte Amalie, in the Virgin Islands.

"The Convent", Formerly "Fernside"

This attractive house was probably built around the turn of the last century. It used to belong to Mr. Cardan Hutchinson and his wife, Georgina, a granddaughter of the famous John Hercules Hazel, founder of Hazells Ltd., who came from one of the Northern Islands. They lived there and raised a large family for many years.

In the late 1920s it was sold to Mrs. Hutchinson's younger brother, Fred Hazel, well known in public life, who became managing director of Hazells Ltd. He died a few years ago. Fred and his wife brought up a family of four lively daughters, one of whom became Mrs. Alec Hughes.

When the family had grown up, Mr. Hazel sold the house to the Nuns of the order of St. Joseph of Cluny, who used part of it for the school they had recently established in Kingstown for children aged five to eleven. The rest of the house was their convent.

Later the school was so successful that new buildings were erected on the site of what had been stables. In the 1970s a secondary school for girls was established. At present there are over three hundred pupils in attendance, as well as five hundred boys and girls in the primary school. Many distinguished people in this island owe part or all their school education to St. Joseph's Convent.

The old house of "Fernside" has not changed much in appearance. A central front door is flanked on each side by two large windows with wooden shutters painted in a cinnamon colour, all heavily shaded by a deep veranda approached by a flight of steps. The roof is of galvanize. This is a very typical design for a tropical house during the fifty years or so before the last war. Verdant lawns shaded by large old trees surround it and the beautiful Mount St. Andrew and other peaks rise up behind. Under the main floor there is much space, some of it now used as a library.

Some readers may not be familiar with the history of the order of St. Joseph of Cluny. Briefly, the Mother Foundress was the daughter of a prosperous farmer near Chambim not far from Paris. She was a teenager in Post Revolutionary France in the early years of the 19th century. At that time the Roman Catholic Church was unpopular with the Revolutionaries and she would help to hide priests in her father's barn as well as secretly giving religious instruction to children.

As an adult, she entered one religious order after another, without finding the exact vocation that she sought. A dream of St. Theresa of Avila, presenting her with a crowd of children of all different races, gave her a goal. She was inspired to give her life to teaching poor children. She left the order in which she was as yet only a novice, and with her two sisters started work among the poor in Paris and then founded the order of St. Joseph.

Premises were made available at Cluny, near Paris. Later she was the first Roman Catholic Missionary to cross the Atlantic to start working in French Guyana at a time just after the abolition of slavery, when much educational and other help was needed to smooth over the momentous social upheaval. The Mother Foundress worked, not only in education of poor children but also in mental hospitals and with lepers. Like so many innovators she had many challenges to overcome with local officialdom.

The order first established a convent in St. Vincent in the 19th century, but the Government of the day was so hostile to Roman Catholicism that they soon left. They returned to Trinidad where their educational efforts were appreciated by the many settlers of

French origin and later by others in that land. Convents were founded in many of the islands. In fact, as many will recall, the order celebrated one hundred and fifty years in the West Indies in 1986.

It was not, however, until 1941 that the sisters returned once more to St. Vincent. Their school is considered one of the first in the nation and they also have a school in the Mesopotamia Valley.

A Survivor

This pleasant white wooden house is a survivor from a number of very attractive homes along Wilson Hill, most of which have been demolished or altered beyond recognition. From the green louvered veranda, there is a clear view through the grassy grounds of the Bishop's College and a vacant lot down into Kingstown's Grenville Street. It was not always so because at one time it faced the large bulk of a fanciful wooden building, adorned with little towers, known as Bishop's Court, once the official residence of the Bishop's

122

of the Windward Islands. From the founding of Bishop's College it became part of the school buildings until its demolition in the early 1970s.

The date of construction of the house, depicted in the sketch, is unknown to me but older residents of Kingstown remember it as far back as 1901.

In 1955, civil servants named the Muiraines, bought it from the Agards. Members of this family have pursued successful careers. Leroy Muiraine, Education Officer, is now the present owner living there with his wife Yvonne, who is acting Head Teacher of the Kingstown Anglican School.

Other brothers and sisters have pursued successful careers in the professions, business and education. Those I have been able to track down include Dr. Carlos Muiraine, St. Vincent's Senior Medical Officer of the Bahamas; Beryl Richards who was Postmaster General up to 1985 and is thought to be the first woman to hold that post in St. Vincent; Bruce, Head Teacher of Sion Hill Government School; Merle, who was Head Teacher in Barrouallie Infant School; a sister who is a teacher in Canada and another brother who is Storekeeper for Federal Chemicals in Trinidad.

An Attractive Home Built By Rosalind (Constantine) Jennings

This attractive house was built around 1926 in typical Kingstown style by Mrs. Jennings (nee Rosalind Constantine) from Calliaqua, while her husband was absent, working with the railways in Nigeria.

The builder was Jim Campbell. At that time it stood on its own extensive grounds with fruit trees, and pastures with cattle, sheep and fowl. The only house nearby was the estate house on top of the little hill where Mr. John Hazell lived for many years.

The house is of plastered stone construction, although the upper story has a wooden gallery partly closed in on the front and supported by arches below. The inside wall of the gallery is painted a beautiful shade of blue.

Enclosed on two sides by the upstairs gallery the spacious living room walls are decorated with a hand painted, coloured design of blurred crossing diagonals, an old and unusual feature. Note the very practical and graceful outside stone staircase, a feature often seen in the older suburban and rural homes.

Mr. Jennings retired in 1932 and the couple lived out their lives in this comfortable home, disturbed only when rioters in the

1930s hid the goods they had stolen from the stores of Kingstown among the bushes near their home.

The house is now the residence of Mrs. Carol Saunders, Mrs. Jennings foster child. Her husband, Mr. James Saunders was a clerk in a business and they had three sons.

The Kingstown Park Guest House

This charming old estate house of stone and wood construction is shown in this two sketches. The wooden louvers of the upper gallery were mostly replaced by glass as the gallery was incorporated into bedrooms.

The house, which is set in a beautiful and convenient location, within walking distance of the center of the city, was built by Alexander Porter at the turn of the 20th century in the midst of Kingstown Park Estate.

Porter, heir to the fabulous D.K. Porter estate, owned twenty-four other estates including Orange Hill, besides his business interests in town and some ships. After his death in 1903, his nephew Jack, who lived in this house and his brother Donald, were the sole beneficiaries of the estate.

Jack a man of reputedly hasty temper, married an Englishwoman and they had a daughter. After the birth of their daughter, Jack sold all his estates, squandered his wealth and returned some years later, alone to St. Vincent. Mr. Casson, the merchant landowner, himself a self-made man, helped him and gave him work. Later Jack went to Barbados where he died. Unfortunately, his brother emigrated to the USA where he also lost his fortune.

Ormond Hazell, a part owner of Mustique Island, bought the house early in the 20th century and his son John Hazell lived and raised his family there for many years.

The home subsequently had several different owners until Nesta Paynter rented it in 1955 as a guesthouse and subsequently bought it. Since that time it has been operating as a pleasant place with constant improvements and sensitive modernizations. The little garden at the back is a delight, with views of the harbour beyond, seen between a brilliant display of tropical plants.

It has been well known for its excellent West Indian style cuisine and many will remember the Halloween dinners offered to collect funds for necessities and comforts at the Mental Health Centre, where Miss Paynter, at one time herself a very active member of the Mental Health Association, used to donate furniture and various improvements to the center.

Miss Paynter was a founder member of many other associations and organizations including the Music Association, where she was an accomplished violinist and guitarist and she volunteered as Treasurer of the Association. She was also a founder member of the Girl Guides Association, the National Trust, the Red Cross and The Netball and Cricket Associations. These were greatly assisted by the special reduced rates she offered for visiting teams for many years in this comfortable guesthouse.

The "Caribbean Bed and Breakfast Book" by Kathy Strong, published by East Woods Press, Charlotte, North Carolina, gives an excellent review of the Kingstown Guest House:

"On a hilltop overlooking the town of Kingstown and granting spectacular views of the sea and emerald green mountains is the personally run guest house owned by Miss Nesta Paynter, a retired civil servant and all round interesting person. At the core of the guest lodgings is the main house, a plantation style structure that

126

was once a prestigious family home. The guests enter through the parlour brimming with antiques, polished wood floors, curios and organdy curtains. A high cathedral ceiling has been painted white and an elegant crystal chandelier hangs from its center. The walls are covered in interesting old photographs taken by the innkeeper herself who, unknown to many, was the first professional lady photographer on the island."

In the 1990s, the guesthouse was converted into a very high class, small hotel with a lovely view and was renamed "Camelot Inn", (which itself has since run into serious financial difficulties).

Traditional Style

The sketch shows an attractive example of a house built in a typical Vincentian, vernacular residential style, which was popular several decades ago. The house is built on McKie's Hill and commands a splendid view of the city and mountains. It was built in 1935 and belongs to the Lewis family who rent it out.

The upper story is of wood and the lower one of stone or concrete. Apparently it was built of excellent materials because it has held up well. Although I have never seen the front door open, I have for pictorial reasons, shown it open with a curtain because I understand that this house does not have the inner swing doors typical of most similar houses.

This residence shows the special West Indian window. The sash window is placed between two wooden panels of movable wooden louvers (or jalousies) let into the wall to give ventilation within even when the windows are closed. To my knowledge, this arrangement is seldom seen outside of the Southern Windward islands. Specifically it resembles the "American Colonial" style buildings where sash windows are flanked by movable louvered shutters hinged to the sides of the windows that have been hooked back (in an open position) to the outside wall on each side of the window.

Worth noticing is the complicated roof structure trimmed with white gingerbread fretwork. This pretty appearance contrasts well with the wild appearance of the jagged dark green mountain peaks behind. There are now only a few buildings left of this old traditional style.

A Pretty House on the Outskirts of Kingstown

Here is a very pretty house on the outskirts of Kingstown, with a wooden upper story on a concrete base. Construction date was probably in the late 1930s or 1940s. The house is rented to tenants by its absentee owner.

At one time there were many houses of this type in the outer residential sections, but the public's desire for more space and easier maintenance has led to the gradual replacement of many. In earlier times it was cheaper to build from the excellent lumber that used to be imported. At present, however, I am told that the costs of building a wooden home are not very different from the costs associated with a more durable concrete house.

This particular house is decorated with pretty white fretwork and the balcony rail is of intricately designed "gingerbread", although it seems to me, more reminiscent of lace trimming. The "gingerbread" design had not been used for at least thirty or forty years until its recent revival in Bequia. The interesting use however, of decorative concrete blocks is seen in many modern homes throughout the nation. It is perhaps a logical evolution from the "gingerbread" style by people who love to beautify their homes.

There is another distinctive feature of this house; that is the arrangement of a sash window. It is flanked by wooden jalousies on each side that are fixed into the wall to allow greater air circulation. A wooden version of this arrangement is sometimes seen, in which the wooden jalousies are replaced with narrow louvered glass windows. To my knowledge this exact window arrangement is not seen outside the West Indies, where it is predominant in the Windward Islands.

The charming house illustrated, enjoys a spectacular view of the city, harbour and surrounding mountains and it is surviving into the twenty-first century although now much obscured at the time of writing by a large Mango tree.

A Hillside Home

This pretty white house of wooden construction is steeply situated on the corner of Long Wall and Kingstown Hill. It was built about 75 years ago by Vincent Frederick on land which he owned. He sold it to Joseph Trotman of Frenches Gate, whose son is now the owner of Trotman's Electronics. The two Trotman daughters inherited the house.

For the past eight years it has been the home of Miss Sylvia Hall and family. The house is daintily trimmed with lacy white fretwork. The sash window below the side gable is flanked in the West Indian manner with dark-green wooden louvers fixed into the wall. Behind this window is a covered gallery enclosed in the gable side, but open at the back for the whole width of the house. It cannot be seen in this sketch and it overlooks the harbour. You will notice a very high pole to which a large number of wires are connected high up in all directions, which is indeed unfortunate for the residents.

Park Lodge on Victoria Park and a Replica in Kingstown Park

"SUNNINGDALE" KINGSTOWN PARK No. 4

"PARK LODGE" ON N.SIDE VICTORIA PK

"Park Lodge" is situated on Victoria Park. Though similar to the "Deanery", it was built considerably earlier and can clearly be seen in a picture at Government House in which Victoria Park is covered with military tents. It used to be a parade ground before it became a pleasure park in honour of the 50th anniversary of Queen Victoria's long reign. It has continued the Royal tradition, with coronations of Carnival Queens and Kings and Queens of the Band and Calypso Kings, not to mention the wonderful performances of the St. Vincent Royal Police Force and once the visit of our gracious reigning Queen Elizabeth. I believe this house was built sometime in the first half of the 19th century. It stood on the present site of Gibson's Building Supplies.

Note its compact, simple but pleasant design and proportions, trimmed with fretwork and with a pretty curved gate. It is not known who built the house but it was probably built for an overseer of the surrounding estate. Dr. Cyril Durrant, the surgeon at the hospital bought the house from Judge St. Aubyn probably in the early part of the last century and his daughter, Kathleen Durrant a former civil servant and secretary of the St. Vincent Red Cross resided there.

To the West of "Park Lodge" there is now a modern Seventh Day Adventist School on the site of the Deanery's former tennis court.

Leaving Victoria Park for a moment, "Sunningdale" which stands in a commanding position on a green hill in Kingstown Park,

132

was built in the 1920s or early 1930s for members of the Richards family. It was said to be a replica of Park Lodge, but actually it is not an exact duplicate. At present the lower gallery looks much taller because the railing has been removed. In recent years it has been used for religious purposes and has been much changed.

Another Decorative Hillside Residence

As is so often seen in St. Vincent's mountainous terrain, the front door of this house leads right into the top story. The hillside to which this building clings is so steep that there is a lower story lying beneath the delicate looking upstairs gallery that runs the whole length of the back of the house.

This is the residence of Mrs. Cora Matthews, on the corner between Long Wall and Town Hill and the road leading up to Cane Garden. Like its neighbour it is built of wood and painted white. There is a trimming of dark red at the corners and the gallery rail. This house is also embellished with lacy white fretwork. The back veranda extends to part of one side, giving a wonderfully airy

133

appearance to the house as seen from the road. One can view ships far out on the sea between the gallery pillars.

Bridges of Kingstown

Kingstown is endowed with some charming little bridges. One of the most attractive is shown in this sketch. It lies between the library garden and the former "Heron" hotel and carries Middle Street as it gracefully arches over the little South River from which that Hotel used to take the name of "Southbridge Hotel". The view is as seen from the back steps of the hotel.

The bridge is painted white and the many uprights, holding up the stone handrails, have the appearance of neatly cut, almost square stones, placed one above the other with very deep indentations between each. This simple and classical form of decoration, known as "Buginato" in Italy gives the bridge an elegant appearance. The long white bridge carrying Back St. over the North River is built in the same style.

The "Buginato" effect is also seen on several other smaller bridges in the city, near the Market, for example, and near Barclays Bank (Halifax St Branch) where unfortunately a damaged upright was recently replaced by a completely plain one, painted white. It lacks any of the "Buginato" indentations which could easily have been made into the concrete in order to harmonise with the others beside it.

"Buginato" effects may be seen on a larger scale in some buildings of the city, especially on the pillars of the Das building.

The Passing of a Landmark

It is sad but true that many interesting buildings vanish without a trace, often without even any pictorial record and worst of all, little public recollection of their appearance. This is even more noticeable in the case of trees, which beautify any village or city.

In 1983 both of the decorative shade giving Eucalyptus trees on the lower part of the Murray road had to be felled. These trees, natives of Australia, were planted around 1905 by the old Agricultural and Horticulture School. They were distinguished by bark with patches of cream, beige and brown and a tall elegant shape and foliage of bluish green colour.

The most dramatic example was the very tall erect tree that stood like a sentinel beside the bridge by the Girls High School. The soaring trunk was rather special because of its bizarre spiral twist, emphasised by the pattern of variegated cream and beige patches on the bark. Because of interference with high-tension wires this fine landmark had to be cut down. One solitary Eucalyptus tree remains beside the Murray Road in front of the Memorial Hall to remind us of the past beauties.

Fortunately beautiful Poui trees with their sudden short lived burst of glory into a mass of brilliant yellow flowers, still stand nearby.

I was pleased that in 1983, the Forestry Department planted young trees of several different decorative varieties along the Murray Road. I expect this lovely approach to the city will be as beautiful as before.

St. Vincent is fortunate in having a Forestry Department, which in addition to its more utilitarian functions, is apparently dedicated to the beautification of the environment.We should not take the department for granted however; they deserve our utmost encouragement and appreciation for their persistent efforts.

A Little Gem of West Indian Archicture

One of the prettiest homes of Kingstown stands on Town Hill. The narrow road is so steep as it climbs out of town, that this house seldom gets the appreciation it deserves, from the many people who plod or drive laboriously up that hill.

The house is of a typically West Indian style developed in the first half of the twentieth century. The steeply gabled, red galvanized roof is trimmed with a lacy white fretwork edging. The house is said to have been built fifty or so years ago.

There is a veranda above and below on the street side. The most charming feature of the house is the upstairs gallery with intricate patterns of crossed pieces of wood forming the ornate balustrade, and a smaller more delicate pattern adorns the gallery just below the white fretwork edging of the roof. There is a graceful outside staircase of stone.

This house is the property of the Williams family, and at present it is rented out. In the past, trucks and vans were prohibited from using that steep, narrow, one-way street. Now, however, even very huge trucks roar up in noisy low gear, which must be most unpleasant for the residents.

An Ornate West Indian House

For over one hundred years, this typical West Indian house has stood opposite the gates to the oldest Botanic Gardens in the Western Hemisphere. Apart from some minor alterations the house remains essentially the same as when I first saw it in the 1950s. This drawing is from that period.

The colour scheme has remained unchanged with the dark maroon coloured wooden walls of the upper story above a whitewashed stone and brick ground floor. The old shingles on the roof have been replaced by galvanized roofing. The house is lavishly trimmed with decorative white "gingerbread" fretwork edgings. The front balcony was once open with a balustrade similar to that seen beside the outside stone staircase and on the balcony at the back.

It was a common practice in the 1940s and 1950s and perhaps earlier for householders to glass in their rather narrow old-fashioned balconies to protect themselves from wind and rain. The front balcony of this house has been completely enclosed. In more modern houses, wooden balconies are unusual and balconies and porches are much wider so that they are not so subject to the elements and therefore can be left open.

All the windows of the house including those behind the glassed in area, are traditional sash windows. Notice the triangular protective pieces of trelliswork flanking the two upstairs windows near the steps with their wide windowsills.

The house is thought to have been built by an off island magistrate called Mr. Isaacs. His son, the late Mr. Conrad Baber Isaacs, born towards the end of the 19th century, inherited the house and lived there for many years. He was a meticulous worker in the Government Audit Department. Later, he became secretary of the Arrowroot pool, where he was of inestimable value, as he was scrupulously careful and absolutely honest. He was noted for his compulsive care of the Arrowroot Pool's Keys. In those days arrowroot experts were vital to St. Vincent's economy. He was most devoted to his mother and did not marry.

In 1977 the Baptist Church purchased the property. The upstairs is used for various cultural activities including those of the then "Triumphant Steel Band" and the ground floor is the headquarters of the "Emerald Group". This Church also runs a preschool for thirty children up to the age of four. The actual church is in the grounds and the Rev. McDowall is the present incumbent minister.

Ness Cottage

Ness Cottage, Sion Hill

Although named a "Cottage", this sketch shows a spacious white wooden house, with lovely views of the city, set on the upper part of Sion Hill. The windows in the front part are closely shuttered and those of the back part are sash windows. It has a quaint little gable over the front door, approached by a double flight of stone steps and there is a pretty little dormer window in the roof. They are both decorated with lacy white fretwork. On the long side facing away from Kingstown, there is another door with a little porch, with a curved roof covered with scalloped shingles, with another double flight of stone steps. In front of this is an elaborate low, stone wall. The lower part of the house is painted black.

At present this house is the "Bahai Centre", the local headquarters for that gentle faith that originated in the last century in Iran. It will be remembered that its followers are now being cruelly persecuted in Iran.

"Ness Cottage" was built or possibly rebuilt by the Scottish wife of the first George Alexander Robertson, soon after they left Richmond Estate following the 1902 Soufriere eruption. For many years they used it as a "Town House" when they were living on their new estate at Campden Park. Later his son George sold it and purchased Fairhall Estate. In the early 1950s this estate was sold to Lewis Punnett, who donated it to the Government and founded the Lewis Punnett Home. After that George Robertson lived in "Ness Cottage" until the time of his death.

Later it became the property of Dr. Harry Munro (who never lived there himself) but from whom the Bahais bought it in the early 1980s.

Diocesan House

This attractive building, with its palladian-style upper windows, stands at the corner of Victoria Park near the main entrance. There is a plaque on it exactly similar to a plaque of the same year, 1806, at the entrance of Fort Charlotte. It is believed to have been built as the Officers Quarters of the British forces garrison stationed in St. Vincent at that time, when the French were a real threat. The house now provides quarters for the Bishop's office and other Diocesan needs, such as accommodation for offices of typist, clerk and the Bishop's Secretary etc. It has been renamed Diocesan House.

Up to quite recently it was the residence of the Archbishop Woodroofe. At first he was Rector of the Cathedral and it was called the Rectory, two years later he was elected Bishop of the Windward Islands and remained in the house. He became Archbishop of the West Indies until he retired from the See in 1986. During that time it was known, appropriately enough, as "Bishop's House."

During its 182 years of life, the house has seen several changes. For example in the 1920s the church council minutes note the gratitude of the Archdeacon, then resident there, for a great advance in sanitary arrangements i.e., a bucket arrangement having been installed in the home instead of the inconvenience of outside sanitation. A chapel has been made in one of the outhouses. At one time it was the residence of the physicist, Archdeacon Maxwell.

Through old age the floor of the upper landing collapsed and fell through in 1984. This was not replaced and instead a circular space was railed around giving a special, graceful, airy effect from the ground floor. Visitors can now stand on the ground floor and look right above. It is said that a ghost lady in a pink negligee used to walk across the upper floor from the east door to the west bedroom. It is not known whether she now walks, or floats across an empty space.

The Museum in the Botanical Gardens

This pretty cottage type house stands inside the Botanical Gardens. It was built for the Curator in 1891. The design was admired enough by some official long ago for him to recommend it as a standard design for Government officials housing. It is indeed a comfortable house, more spacious within than one might suppose. The post of Curator was usually combined with that of Superintendent of Agriculture.

Some of those who held the post, included T.P. Jackson, C.K. Robertson, Mike Hanchell and the last superintendent who lived in the house, a Vincentian, Hugh McConnie and his wife Patricia. The large porch, so often the venue for delightful parties, used to be decorated with white fretwork, but when this deteriorated it was replaced with decorated blocks, which seem to be the modern and more durable equivalent.

There was a beautiful garden filled with brilliant flowers in front of the house and the approach was under two arched arbours of dark blue wild pea. After Mr. McConnie was directed by the then Governor to vacate the house in the early 1970s, so that it could be converted into a museum, the garden was simplified into a plain lawn.

In 1979 the museum was opened, mainly due to the enthusiastic energy of Dr. Earl Kirby, a professional veterinarian (now retired), but at heart, an archaeologist and historian. This was a project of the St. Vincent National Trust and Dr. Kirby. Kirby was helped by Mrs. Barbara Wall, who contributed some very fine objects she had discovered by herself and others.

This museum is well known and contains a wonderful collection of "Pre-Columbian artifacts" consisting of the remains of objects used by Caribs and other people who inhabited this island countless ages before it was settled by people from the other side of the Atlantic Ocean.

The museum is open on Wednesdays 8:30am to 12:00 midday and Saturdays 4am - 6pm.

144

Government House

This sketch shows Government House set on a verdant hillside below a wooded crag above the Botanic Gardens. The house is of white shingle clad wood construction with three large fretwork-trimmed gables above a base of bricks and concrete. There are many additions to the back and sides. This residence commands a beautiful view of the Grenadines and on a clear day one can even see Grenada.

A wide straight flight of stone or concrete steps leads straight down through its own lovely landscaped grounds into the Botanic Gardens.

In earlier days when Carnival was smaller, the Carnival bands used to go up to Government House and show off their costumes and music to the Administrator or the Governor. At the end of the last century St. Vincent was headed by a Lieutenant Governor working under the Governor of the Windward Islands in Grenada.

Later this office was abolished and an Administrator lived in Government House and performed the same functions. When the Governor of the Windward Islands came to St. Vincent on one of his periodic official visits, the Administrator would vacate Government House for the Governor.

When St. Vincent achieved Statehood in 1969, the Administrator, Hywell George, from Britain, was appointed as Governor of St. Vincent by the Queen, at the request of Premier,

Milton Cato. He was followed from 1970 to 1976, by Sir Rupert John, (the first Vincentian to hold that post). Sir Rupert, was succeeded by Sir Sidney Gun-Munro, a Grenadian, who had worked long years as a most popular and dedicated Senior Surgeon at Kingstown General Hospital.

The Administrator post was renamed "Governor General" at Independence in 1979. Sir Sidney retired in 1985 to live a quiet life with his English born wife, Joan, in Bequia, rearing a variety of domestic and farm animals and birds. During his term of office he founded the important Children's Welfare Fund.

Sir Sidney was succeeded as Acting Governor General by Sir Lambert Eustace, who was himself, succeeded by the eminent lawyer Mr. Henry Williams.

Beneath the three gables of the house are numerous windows. I suspect that once they were open verandas running along the front, but were glassed in later to protect against driving rain. The roofs are galvanized.

According to Charles Shephard's "Historical Account to the Island of St. Vincent" first published in 1831, the thirty-acre Botanical Gardens, which had been successfully established in 1763 had deteriorated after the death of Superintendent Lockhead in 1814. His successor was a very dissatisfied person who apparently did incompetent work.

The legislature expended eight hundred pounds annually to partially maintain the gardens and preserve the remaining trees, but this money was discontinued in 1828 and four thousand, five hundred pounds was voted to the Governor, Sir Charles Brisbane to erect a "Cottage". It was completed and "three acres of the gardens were conveyed to the trustees for the Governor's use." This was said to be "for the time being" because of the old Government House in Kingstown having long been in a dilapidated state.

Where that house was is uncertain, but I suspect that it may still exist in the much renovated, old brick Government offices building. The Georgian style of architecture, with well spaced sash windows and the elegant details of some of the upstairs rooms, before they were divided up to make more offices, would fit the period between the end of the 19th century and first part of the 20th century. An alternative theory of course, is that it might have been completely demolished.

Whether the "cottage" built in 1828 for the Governor was similar to the present Government House, or whether it was rebuilt on a larger and more appropriate scale at a later date, I have not been able to ascertain. It certainly does not resemble a "Cottage" size and yet the style is unpretentious and the fretwork trimmed gables reminiscent of cottage style architecture, yet on an unusually large scale. A main internal feature is a large lofty central hall, running from front to back, where receptions were held.

In 1881 the Duke of York, who later became King George V of England, visited St. Vincent and he remarked on the building recommending that it undergo repair. This was done in 1885. Probably its appearance after those repairs was much as it is now without the additions and the glassing in of the verandas. It is indeed strange that one Government House after another should have been allowed to get into such bad condition. Perhaps the planters who sat on the Legislative Council felt disinclined to vote enough money for maintenance in the hard economic times at the end of the 19th century.

Winsor, An Attractive Old House

This attractive old house stands on terraced grounds bordered by retaining walls on the very steep hillside that rises on the Southern edge of Kingstown.

Winsor is soon to pass out of the hands of the descendants of the Fraser family that has owned it since 1935 and doubtless its function will change from that of a private home for a large family to some other use.

John Gregg Winsor Hazell is the great grandson of the founder of the Hazel family of Bequia. Hercules Hazell (1733-1833), and son of the John Hercules Hazel (1817-1886) who founded the precursor of Hazells Ltd., bought or inherited Winsor house. He lived from 1848-1915 and had 12 children, one of whom was Alfred Gregg Hazel (1891-1971) a distinguished citizen and Managing Director of Hazells for many years, to whom he bequeathed the house. Mass Fred, as he was generally known, moved to "Fernside" (now the convent) and sold Winsor to Stanley DeFreitas the lawyer in 1935 who in turn sold it to Mr. A.M. Fraser.

In 1944 the schooner, "Island Queen" vanished on a voyage from Grenada to St. Vincent. Many Vincentians perished, including two of Mr. Fraser's children. After this tragedy, he brought his remaining family from Ruthland Vale (near Layou) to live at Winsor.

The house is of white painted wood on a masonry base with red galvanised roofing. It was probably constructed in the second half of the 19th century, or possibly earlier. The roof was blown off in the 1898 hurricane. There is a long central portion with a gallery flanked by "bow windows" at each end. The front door is centrally placed and approached by a graceful semicircular staircase. There is a masonry basement beneath its single wooden story. This part of the house is of a design often seen in the West Indies, but Winsor is remarkable in having two smaller two story buildings attached to each side by corridors. One suspects that these were later additions as the family grew.

At present it is not possible for a vehicle to come up to the house; it has to be left below two walled terraces and the house is reached by a long broad flight of steps leading on to the so called "Horsewalk". In the old days after being released from the carriage, the horses were led up two shallow steps on to this ramp, heavily scored in a checked pattern to prevent them slipping, until they reached the level of the house where they turned left, below the gallery of the small left hand wing, on their way to the stables.

Behind the house is a courtyard above which rises narrow, terraced gardens, shaded by fruit trees. Behind these, the land rises almost vertically, shrouded with a luxuriant and impenetrable tropical jungle until it reaches civilization again on the plateau of suburban Cane Garden far above.

The Handsome Home of a Talented Family

This attractive house with its unusually large sash windows used to stand on the corner of Higginson Street opposite the Methodist Church, and Back Street opposite the Anglican Catherdral which can be glimpsed in this sketch. The drawing only shows the Higginson Street side of this large house which can easily be seen from Back Street.

The land upon which it stood used to belong to a Methodist minister, the Rev. Simmon Bacchus who died in Tortola. His widow, Mrs. Leonora Bacchus, erected this house around the turn of the last century. The niece of the minister. Louise Bacchus, used to live in the house when she was one of the first pupils of the Girl's High

School when it opened in 1911 in a small house on Victoria Park. Later she married Mr. Wilberforce Prescod who later became Headmaster of Georgetown School and then Inspector of Schools for the entire island.

The Prescods rented the house after the death of Mrs. Prescod's aunt (Leonora Bacchus) and the immigration of her daughter to the US. After the second world war, Mr. Prescod bought the house. From then to this day, it has been a hive of musical and commercial educational activity.

Mr. Prescod started a most successful school for commercial subjects including typing and shorthand. The school is presently run by his daughter Cynthia.

Mrs. Louise Prescod had started teaching piano prior to her marriage and at the time of writing, she still continues to take many pupils as she has for over 60 years.

The renowned organist, Pat Prescod brilliantly carries on the musical traditions of this dignified looking house.

The North River Road and McCoy Street

Here is a view of the lower part of the North River which few will have stopped to notice.

On the other side of the river is empty land, usually covered with grass and with wires set up for drying, washing and repairing fishnets. This area is partly shaded by one of the few trees of Kingstown, a magnificent Flamboyant with pale green feathery leaves, long brown pods , and in season, huge clusters of scarlet flowers.

Beyond this McCoy Street runs gently up hill between Bay St. and Back St. The houses form a pleasant row, although it is sad to see the disrepair of the first one on the right. The next one has a pretty upstairs gallery. The next structure has been rebuilt in the last few months following the actual creation of the sketch. After the next very small building comes a large simple building. The tower of the Anglican Church can be seen behind.

On the opposite side of Back St. is "Reesbank", in classic Kingstown style. This house is painted white and was for many years the Connell residence. The arched gallery dates from as early as the 1930's.

Reesbank once housed the very first dress boutique of the city and was opened by Mrs. Antrobus under the name of "La Boutique". At one time it also housed the SPCK Bookshop famous for its selection of school and other books. Later it was the home of Eustace Auto Supplies.

Behind "Reesbank" rise the beautiful ornate towers of the Roman Catholic St. Mary's Presbytery and Co-Cathedral of the Assumption.

The boat in the foreground was in that position, presumable for repainting, when the sketch was made. The beach with its many fishing boats is nearby.

A FINAL NOTE TO MY READERS

I am pleased you have accompanied me on this illustrated journey through Kingstown, the capital of St. Vincent & the Grenadines. My notes and sketches are inconclusive, but hopefully they have stirred the memories of our senior citizens, interested our many tourists and visitors and helped all of us to better understand how our beautiful city has evolved.

Time marches on. During the balance of the twenty-first century, hurricanes, volcanic activity, fires and the destructive hammers of developers and builders will have turned many more of our distinctive landmarks into distant memories recorded only in the minds of our seniors and in the archives of history.

The past is history: We cannot change what has been, but we can learn from our successes and our failures. The present is today: By creating a national awareness and sensitivity of our culture and our history, we can preserve our remaining icons of historical significance for the future, which is tomorrow. Failure to do so will create an unforgiveable and irreplacable loss to future generations

INDEX

Other Works by Dr. Vivian Child
Puffy and Buttons
ISBN 0-533-09365-1
Published by: Vantage Press Inc. New York City USA

To be released mid year 2004
"To an Island in Africa
 Working, Walking, and Painting in Tanzania, 1951-1954
by Dr. Vivian Usborne Child as told to Julie Savage Lea"
ISBN 1-4134-4214-5 Hardcover edition
ISBN 1-4134-4213-7 2004 Paperback
Published by: Xlibris of Philadelphia, Pennsylvania, USA

Printed in the United States
19742LVS00002B/7-86